Abstract Expressionism:
Works on Paper

Abstract Expressionism: Works on Paper

Selections from The Metropolitan Museum of Art

Lisa Mintz Messinger

The Metropolitan Museum of Art, New York

High Museum of Art, Atlanta

Distributed by Harry N. Abrams, Inc., New York

This volume has been published in conjunction with the exhibition "Abstract Expressionism: Works on Paper," held at the High Museum of Art, Atlanta, from January 26, 1993, through April 4, 1993, and at The Metropolitan Museum of Art from May 4, 1993, through September 12, 1993.

The exhibition catalogue is made possible, in part, by funds from the Fay and George Owen Sheffield Memorial Endowment of the High Museum of Art.

Published by The Metropolitan Museum of Art, New York, and the High Museum of Art, Atlanta

John P. O'Neill, Editor in Chief
Barbara Cavaliere, Editor
Steffie Kaplan, Designer
Peter Antony, Production

Library of Congress Cataloging-in-Publication Data

Metropolitan Museum of Art (New York, N.Y.)
    Abstract expressionism: works on paper: selections from the
Metropolitan Museum of Art/by Lisa Mintz Messinger.
        p.   cm.
    Exhibition catalog.
    Includes bibliographical references and index
    ISBN 0-87099-656-8.—ISBN 0-87099-657-6 (PbK).—ISBN 0-8109-6424-4
(Abrams)
    1. Abstract expressionism—United States—Exhibitions.   2. Art.
American—Exhibitions.   3. Small art works—20th century—United
States—Exhibitions.   4. Metropolitan Museum of Art (New York,
N.Y.)—Exhibitions.   I. Messinger, Lisa Mintz.   II. Title.
N6512.5.A25M48   1993
759. 13'09'040747471—dc20   92-33802
                                                                CIP

All photographs by The Photograph Studio, The Metropolitan Museum of Art

Composition by U.S. Lithograph, typographers, New York
Printed by Mercantile Printing Company, Worcester, Massachusetts
Bound by Acme Bookbinding Company, Charlestown, Massachusetts

Jacket/cover: Willem de Kooning, *Zot* (cat. no. 8)

Contents

Acknowledgments

Many people at the Museum have contributed to various aspects of this publication, and my thanks go to all of them for helping to bring it to fruition. In particular, I would like to thank John P. O'Neill, Editor in Chief, whose advice at every stage of the book's development was of great value; Barbara Cavaliere, editor of this volume, whose own expertise in the subject provided a wealth of information and critical judgment; Steffie Kaplan for her elegant design; Peter Antony for his intelligent direction of the book's production; Margaret Holben Ellis and Peter Bornstein of the Department of Paper Conservation, whose immense knowledge of media and techniques was the source for much of the catalogue's technical discussion; and Patti Stuckler, Graduate Intern at the Museum during the Summer of 1990, who assembled the initial source material for the text.

The exhibition that this catalogue accompanies was the idea of William S. Lieberman, Jacques and Natasha Gelman Chairman of the Department of 20th Century Art at The Metropolitan Museum of Art, and I thank him for allowing me to develop the project. As always, his advice and support have been invaluable. Ida Balboul, Jennifer Ball, Kay Bearman, and Lowery S. Sims, all of the Department of 20th Century Art, also deserve my thanks for their contributions to the preparation of the catalogue and the exhibition.

Finally, I would like to acknowledge the role of the High Museum of Art, Atlanta, Georgia, as co-publisher of the catalogue and as a participant in the exhibition tour. It was through the initial efforts of Gudmund Vigtel, Director Emeritus of the High Museum of Art, and Naomi Vine, former Associate Director of the High, that the Metropolitan agreed to organize this catalogue and the exhibition it accompanies, and through the continued commitment of Ned Rifkin, Director of the High, and Carrie Przybilla, Associate Curator of 20th Century Art at the High, the project has been realized.

Lisa Mintz Messinger
Assistant Curator, Department of 20th Century Art
The Metropolitan Museum of Art

Foreword

The Metropolitan Museum of Art has a strong commitment to Abstract Expressionism and is fortunate to have a superb collection of paintings and works on paper by the major participants in this important movement in twentieth-century art. Many of the Museum's large canvases were purchased during the 1950s, shortly after they were painted, on the advice of Robert Beverly Hale, who was then the Museum's curator of 20th Century Art. Under the subsequent curatorships of Henry Geldzahler, Thomas B. Hess, and William S. Lieberman, many additional works have been acquired through purchase, gift, and bequest. Most of the Museum's Abstract Expressionist works on paper are more recent acquisitions, attained primarily through the generosity of the artists themselves, their families, and a few dedicated collectors. Of the sixty works in this selection, forty-four have entered the Metropolitan's collection since 1982, and the promised gifts of Muriel Kallis Newman made during that year include a number of significant paintings and works on paper, four of which appear in this publication and in the exhibition that it accompanies.

The major strength of the Museum's collection of Abstract Expressionist works on paper is the depth of its holdings of some of the central figures of the group. Willem de Kooning is represented by eight works, Mark Rothko by nine, and Jackson Pollock by forty-one, in addition to seventy-one sketches in the three notebooks purchased by the Museum in 1990.

The publication of this catalogue continues the Museum's ongoing mission to document works in its permanent collection. It also marks the first time a major museum has brought together a group of works on paper by these artists, most of whom are best known for their large-scale painted works. It is hoped that this selection will lead to new insights into the accomplishments of the Abstract Expressionists by concentrating on their smaller and more intimate creations.

The Metropolitan Museum is pleased to acknowledge the High Museum of Art, Atlanta, Georgia, for its important contribution to the realization of this project. It is from the High's initial interest in pursuing a joint venture between the two museums that this exhibition and catalogue developed. Continued collaboration has resulted in the copublication of this volume by both museums and the presentation of the exhibition at the High Museum prior to its installation at the Metropolitan.

Philippe de Montebello
Director
The Metropolitan Museum of Art

Foreword

The High Museum of Art is proud to have initiated this joint venture with The Metropolitan Museum of Art. The collections of the Metropolitan are enviable for their range and depth in many areas; this exhibition of works on paper by artists associated with Abstract Expressionism is but one example. We are delighted to present these important yet seldom-seen works for the first time outside of New York. They provide rare insight into the artists' thought processes and working methods, and offer a striking complement to the High's holdings of postwar art. We thank the Metropolitan for sharing its collections with Atlanta audiences and are pleased to copublish this catalogue for the occasion. It is an important scholarly document as well as a testament to the success of this partnership.

Ned Rifkin
Director
High Museum of Art

Introduction

In New York City in the early 1940s, a few small groups of artists from varied backgrounds began working toward an abstract art that could express a subject matter relevant to such dark times. They followed no single stylistic agenda but shared a conviction that art must express the universal truths generated by the most deeply personal inner experiences. With the atrocities of World War II raising questions about humanity's place in the world, these artists developed a global awareness stimulated by many diverse and overlapping sources—among them, European modernist art, primitive art, mythology, psychology, and the mystical belief systems and art of the East. What they developed during the 1940s has come to be known as Abstract Expressionism, one of the century's most important and influential artistic movements. Many articles and books have been published about these artists, both individually and as a group, and the variety of interpretations these texts present ranges from the poetic to the scholarly. One of the most sustaining qualities of Abstract Expressionist art is its ability to evoke many possible associations and interpretations. During the past fifty years, the preeminence of the movement in post-World War II art has been firmly established in the annals of art history. Yet the Abstract Expressionists and the innovative works they created still defy definitive classification.

The large-scale paintings and sculptures these artists began to make during the late 1940s gained prominence during the 1950s and have continued to command great attention. During the past ten years, however, serious notice has been given to their works of the early to mid–1940s, the period during which they were synthesizing their ideas from a range of visual and conceptual sources. Rarely have the Abstract Expressionists been considered as a group through their works on paper, although most of them worked prolifically in this area. Their extensive bodies of work on paper provide key insights into both their shared intentions and their individual routes toward mature expression.

Most of the Abstract Expressionists made numerous works on paper during the 1940s, when they were experimenting with new formal structures and imagery. Jackson Pollock created hundreds of sketches on his way to finding a unique synthesis of drawing and painting in the large drip and spatter paintings he began to make in 1947. David Smith, closely paralleling the researches of Pollock, relied on drawing to develop the forms for his sculptures, which, in fact, have been called "drawings in the air." The sculptor Theodore Roszak, on the other hand, made drawings as preliminary sketches for his metal pieces. Franz Kline used enlargements of his sketches as the basis for his sweeping black-and-white paintings. Arshile Gorky preferred to draw directly from nature, and he often rearranged elements of those drawings in composing his paintings. From his student days, Willem de Kooning was a masterful draftsman, and he continued to draw prodigiously as he moved through biomorphism and further into abstraction.

For de Kooning, Kline, and Pollock, the route to their innovative paintings was directly through drawing. What they created was a painterly sweeping motion that breaks down the traditional boundaries of these two media. Their paintings became more direct as they progressed, but they continued to make sketches on paper, more often as a way to loosen up and further evolve their imagery than to produce finished works. De Kooning, for example, who has continued to draw extensively, made a series of rapidly executed and roughly indicated twisting figures in charcoal on typewriter paper during the 1980s that demonstrate drawing's ongoing importance for him.

For other Abstract Expressionist artists, drawing was primarily a means to discover painterly qualities that could better express their multireferential content. During the 1940s, Mark Rothko worked mostly in watercolor, a medium particularly important for his development of evocative forms in layered light-filled surfaces. As his work matured into more abstract and simplified imagery, he made fewer works on paper, and those that exist are smaller versions of the paintings. During the 1940s, Theodoros Stamos created numerous works on paper, often in mixed media, in which his biomorphic imagery and scumbled layered surfaces are well exemplified. The papers made over the years by Richard Pousette-Dart and Adolph Gottlieb are, like those by Stamos, independent paintings on paper in which the artists discover the colors and forms that will be shifted and relocated on their larger canvases. For Barnett Newman, drawing was particularly important during the 1940s. His works on paper provide a comprehensive record of his evolution through organic form to his drastically simplified later works, and these small pieces are crucial for understanding the essential meaning of his art. Philip Guston also relied specifically on drawing to develop the visual repertoire in both his Abstract Expressionist paintings and his later, more figural works. James Brooks's drawings, on the other hand, echo the imagery he had already developed in his paintings.

During the early 1940s, William Baziotes and Robert Motherwell blended Surrealist techniques with Cubist formal elements to create works that fulfill the idea expressed by Motherwell in 1944 as "plastic automatism." For a brief time during that period, Gerome Kamrowski made complex and highly inventive works on paper that demonstrate his contribution to the early development of that idea, before his work led him in a direction that separates him from subsequent Abstract Expressionist art. Baziotes made many papers throughout his career, and they provide a revealing look at his evolution from allover layered compositions with multiple forms to subtle translucent surfaces inhabited by singular multireferential images. His masterful watercolors of the 1950s are small gems that reflect the shimmering light in his larger pictures.

Anne Ryan and Mark Tobey both worked almost exclusively on paper and on a small scale. Along with Kamrowski, they exemplify the artists of the period whose works on paper in a variety of media relate to Abstract Expressionist art: both Ryan's and Tobey's works in formal structure and Tobey's in significative content as well.

Three seminal Abstract Expressionist painters—Ad Reinhardt, Clyfford Still, and Bradley Walker Tomlin—are represented at the Museum only by paintings on canvas, thus precluding their inclusion in this selection. Reinhardt's best-known works on paper are abstract collages and gouaches of 1939 to 1950 and several satirical collaged cartoons that comment on the art world. Still made pastels and oil and gouache paintings on paper in which he explored compositions and imagery for his large-scale paintings on canvas. Tomlin's works on paper are relatively unknown. Lee Krasner is also absent from this selection; her works on paper in the Museum's collection are cubistic analyses she made from 1937 to 1940, when she was a student of Hans Hofmann's. Some of the artists included in this publication are represented in the Museum's collection by several works on paper. Choices were made, for example, from among the Museum's eight papers by Willem de Kooning, forty-one by Jackson Pollock (plus seventy-one sketches by him in three notebooks), and nine by Mark Rothko.

The great variety of media and materials used by these artists indicates both their nontraditionalist attitude and their poverty. It was most likely a combination of these two factors that motivated Pollock, for example, to use bank forms for sketching, or that led Kline to work on pages from newspapers and telephone books. Elaine de Kooning spoke about how lack of funds made it necessary for her to use brown wrapping paper for her 1948 series of drawings. Most of the Abstract Expressionists were extremely poor, and many remained so throughout most of their lives. Proud of their stance as outsiders, they willingly used nontraditional materials and techniques in both small and large works. Immediacy and directness were major concerns in the Abstract Expressionists' search for externalization of innermost emotions, and small-scale works on paper provided a means to explore and experiment and to react spontaneously on an intimate scale. Preserved on paper are the records of their struggle to find, continually renew, and further advance the visual expression of their revolutionary ideas.

William Baziotes
1912—1963

1. *Florida Seascape,* 1945
Gouache, pen and ink, brush and ink, and
watercolor on paper
14¼ × 19¾ in. (36.2 × 50.2 cm)
George A. Hearn Fund, 1946 (46.72a,b)

2. *Cobra,* 1957
Watercolor and pencil on paper
18⅜ × 24¼ in. (46.7 × 61.6 cm)
Anonymous Gift, in honor of Tullio Lombardo,
1972 (1972.201)

William Baziotes moved from his hometown of Reading,
Pennsylvania, to New York City in August of 1933. He studied at the National Academy of Design until 1936, and during
that year, he was hired by the Works Progress Administration Federal Art Project as a teacher.[1] He began working on
the WPA's Easel Painting Project in 1938, and it was during
the next few years that he met many of his fellow Abstract
Expressionist painters as well as a number of Surrealists,
most important for him, Matta (Roberto Matta Echaurren)
and Gordon Onslow-Ford, both of whom were his age.

Even before he moved to New York, Baziotes had become familiar with Symbolist poetry, and he developed a
lasting affinity with the ideas and work of Charles Baudelaire,
Paul Valéry, and a number of other poets. Their idea of
"correspondences," poetic analogies whereby multiple references are suggested through one form, was of singular importance in the development of Baziotes' art. Among his earliest
visual sources are the works of Pablo Picasso and Joan Miró
from the 1920s and 1930s; both had painted semiabstract images that allowed for various possible interpretations. Stimulated by his friendships with Matta and Onslow-Ford,
Baziotes, in 1940–41, experimented with techniques based
on the Surrealist practice of psychic automatism. In 1941, he
demonstrated some of the possibilities of such techniques
to Jackson Pollock at Gerome Kamrowski's studio. In 1975,

Kamrowski described the event: "Baziotes was enthusiastically talking about the new freedoms and techniques of painting and noticing the quart cans of lacquer asked if he could use some to show Pollock how the paint could be spun around . . . a canvas that I had been pouring paint on . . . was not going well. . . . Bill then began to throw and drip the white paint on the canvas. He handed the palatte [*sic*] knife to Jackson and Jackson with his intense concentration was flipping the paint with abandon."[2] The result of this encounter was a collaborative canvas, which is now in Kamrowski's collection.

In 1941, Matta introduced Baziotes to Robert Motherwell, who also had a strong interest in Surrealism and in Symbolist poetry. The two Americans attempted to organize a group of artists to continue to explore the possibilities of automatism, and although this never materialized, they did disseminate their ideas to their fellow artists. They did not adhere to the automatism practiced by the orthodox Surrealists, but instead conveyed their own idea, which was to create pictures that are more painterly and more abstract and that communicate a subject matter closer to the Symbolist poets' correspondences than to the Surrealists' psychologically based dream imagery. Theirs was an early expression of the idea that lies at the core of Abstract Expressionism. In a 1947 statement titled "I Cannot Evolve any Concrete Theory," Baziotes articulated this idea: "There is no particular system I follow when I begin a painting. Each painting has its own way of evolving. One may start with a few color areas on the canvas; another with a myriad of lines; and perhaps another with a profusion of color. Each beginning suggests something. Once I sense the suggestion, I begin to paint intuitively. The suggestion then becomes a phantom that must be caught and made real. As I work, or when the painting is finished, the subject reveals itself."[3]

Throughout his career from the 1930s until his death in 1961, Baziotes made many drawings, which stand as independent works and are never studies for specific paintings. *Florida Seascape* (fig. 1) was made during the summer of 1945, while Baziotes and his wife, Ethel, were on a three-week vacation in Florida with Motherwell and his first wife, Maria. Their visit to an isolated beach near Saint Augustine, located along the northeast coastline, inspired this churning composition. The drawing marks a brief transitional phase in Baziotes' oeuvre, when he was creating complex multiple forms in an irregular grid format that mark his final synthesis of Surrealist and Cubist elements.[4] The verso of *Florida*

1. *Florida Seascape*, 1945

Seascape (fig. 1a) reveals an early stage in Baziotes' process in which he blocked in the basic outlines of the composition. In the finished work, similar preliminary outlines of black ink and yellow paint are almost completely obliterated by areas of steely-blue and yellow-green paint. In his works on paper of the 1940s, Baziotes experimented with various media; here, mottled translucent watercolor is juxtaposed with flat opaque gouache and dense shiny India ink. He achieved a similar translucency with oil paints, which he diluted considerably in his late paintings. As in many of Baziotes' later drawings, the white page is unpainted in several places and enhances the play on negative-positive space. A wide variety of curving and flowing linear elements either delineate or fracture the myriad shapes and direct the viewer's eyes over this complex composition in continuous, sometimes staccato, motions.

Florida Seascape is filled with undulating biomorphic forms that suggest an array of exotic creatures and plants, some real, some imaginary, which bear a resemblance to Miró's imagery. The allusion to the dark and mysterious world found under the sea also conveys the connections between the diverse levels of life from the primordial past even to the present. Biomorphic forms and marine imagery also appeared in the contemporaneous work of Adolph Gottlieb, Mark Rothko, and Theodoros Stamos. The spidery veins, broken lines, and configurations of varied thickness and direction that unite the many sections of this work add to the underlying sense of convergence. Coexisting with the dark underside, there is also a lighter side; Baziotes' picture is enlivened with humorous associations such as the whimsical meandering dashes that recall the helter-skelter tracks made by birds in the sand along the seashore. Baziotes once remarked: "My work is like the Caribbean—Above the Blue Sky and Below the Blue Water—beneath the sharks."[5] Communicating the duality of nature was central in Baziotes' art for the rest of his life.

Baziotes' work after 1947 retained many of the elements in this earlier work on paper, including his graceful line and the biomorphic imagery that evokes correspondences. As he progressed, the forms become fewer in number, the colors and surfaces subtler, the idea distilled closer to its essence. This simplification is also evident in Baziotes' use of fewer media in his works on paper after 1950, which are most often limited to watercolor with pencil lines. *Cobra* of 1957 (fig. 2) is exemplary of this refinement in which every element of the work is pared down to its essential form.

1a. *Florida Seascape,* 1945 (verso)

On a sheet of textured watercolor paper, which was originally tacked down along its edges, Baziotes penciled the outlines of the two sections of his composition. The long and wiggly form on the left resembles some sort of serpent or worm, and the combination of uneven square and organic shapes on the right suggests a primordial life form. Throughout Baziotes' oeuvre, such forms metamorphose in endless variations and combinations. The imagery in *Cobra* certainly evolves from Baziotes' earlier work, particularly the tentacle-like form and the delicate ovoid that appear within the square. But there is also a relationship with works of art that he saw in museums, interestingly often with sculpture, both ancient and more contemporary. The right-hand section of this work, for example, is evocative of a marble sculpture on a large pedestal, and among many possible connections, there is a visual affinity with works by the British sculptor Henry Moore of the 1930s to the 1950s that incorporate incised circles and radial disks. Moore's work was shown at the Museum of Modern Art and at New York galleries during the 1940s and 1950s, and, like Baziotes, he also had Surrealist affiliations for a time.

While the shapes themselves are unpainted except for a few spots of pale color, the area surrounding them is divided into two horizontal color zones. The bottom third of the surface is an intense aquamarine, and the area above is a mottled wash of olive green that is subtly modulated with shades of brighter green and brown. These closely harmonized halftones are characteristic of Baziotes' late work. His choices of color were meant to enhance the underlying meaning in all his works. In the artist's own words, "I paint with in-between colors. When you look at nature, the colors are in-between, and when you add psychology, they are even more in-between."[6]

In 1947, Harold Rosenberg wrote of Baziotes' work: "The textures seem to absorb silence as if the paints had been mixed in the medium of sleep."[7] A similar reference is found in remarks made by the artist in 1952 in which Baziotes, speaking of "the stillness and silence" in his pictures, noted: "I want my pictures to take effect very slowly, to obsess and haunt."[8] During the 1950s, Baziotes' working method became even slower and more meditative; he produced only one or two oil paintings a year. His works on paper were a quicker, more immediate outlet for developing his vocabulary of forms. They always reflect the intentions formulated during the early 1940s by this early and consistent participant in Abstract Expressionism.

2. *Cobra*, 1957

1. The Works Progress Administration was established by Franklin Delano Roosevelt in 1935. In 1939, when it was made part of the Federal Works Agency, it was renamed the Work Projects Administration.

2. Gerome Kamrowski, quoted from a letter to William Rubin, April 10, 1975; reprinted in Mona Hadler, "William Baziotes: Four Sources of Inspiration," in Newport Harbor Art Museum, *William Baziotes: A Retrospective Exhibition*, exh. cat. (Newport Beach, Ca., 1978), p. 83.

3. William Baziotes, quoted from a statement titled "I Cannot Evolve any Concrete Theory," *Possibilities* 1, no. 1 (Winter 1947–48), p. 2.

4. The structure of *Florida Seascape* is related to oil paintings by Baziotes of 1944 and 1945, such as *The Balcony,* 1944, Collection Wright Ludington; *The Parachutists,* 1944, Collection Estate of William Baziotes; and *Still Life,* 1945, Collection Washington University Gallery of Art, St. Louis.

5. Baziotes, quoted from a conversation with Ethel Baziotes, in *William Baziotes: Paintings and Works on Paper 1952–1961*, exh. cat., Blum Helman Gallery (New York, 1988), p. 15.

6. Baziotes, quoted from an unpublished interview with Donald Paneth, January 1952, p. 8, in Archives of American Art, William Baziotes papers.

7. Harold Rosenberg, quoted from Irving H. Sandler, "Baziotes: Modern Mythologist," *Art News* 63, no. 10 (February 1965), p. 66.

8. Baziotes, quoted from Paneth, p. 7.

James Brooks
1906–1992

3. *Number 4—1960,* 1960
Acrylic and oil on paper
20¾ × 14¾ in. (52.7 × 37.5 cm)
Gift of Charlotte Park Brooks, 1991 (1991.211)

James Brooks's place among the first-generation Abstract Expressionists has sometimes been forgotten or obscured because he was absent from the New York art scene during a critical period in the development and dissemination of Abstract Expressionist ideas. While he was serving as an art correspondent in the United States Army from 1942 until 1945, artists such as William Baziotes, Philip Guston, Robert Motherwell, Jackson Pollock, Ad Reinhardt, and Mark Rothko were beginning to show their work in New York City galleries. Although Brooks rapidly adopted Abstract Expressionist ideas after 1945, his first solo exhibition in New York did not take place until 1950.

When Brooks returned to New York City in September of 1945, he renewed his acquaintance with several Abstract Expressionist artists. Among them are Bradley Walker Tomlin, with whom he had shared a studio in 1931, and Philip Guston and Jackson Pollock, both of whom he had known through the Works Progress Administration in the late 1930s. Brooks abandoned his prewar social realism, and in 1946, he began to make work that aligned him with his Abstract Expressionist colleagues. He continued to pursue these ideals with unflagging persistence throughout the rest of his life and was an active spokesman for them both as a teacher and as a participant in the group's formal and informal discussions.

In 1947, Brooks tried Pollock's techniques of pouring and dripping. Finding they were not for him, he continued, for the next year or two, to experiment with various techniques and media, including the incorporation of collage elements into his painted canvases. This avenue of exploration led to an accidental discovery during the summer of 1948. As Brooks affixed paper to canvas, some of the glue bled through to the back side of the canvas, where it produced an irregular pattern. Brooks was so inspired by these ghostly shapes that he deliberately stained subsequent canvases with diluted paint as a point of departure for further improvisation.[1] This idea evolved to produce paintings in which washes of color are juxtaposed with linear details. Brooks's paintings from the late 1940s and the 1950s are characteristically composed of dense allover surfaces. During this period, he achieved similar effects in his works on paper, which were executed in oil paint or in gouache and which, like his large canvases, combine areas of intense or subtle color with strong counterpoints of black. Divergent effects resulted, however, because of the different qualities of canvas and paper. The thin washes of color seep into the unsized canvas fabric and bleed together to give Brooks's paintings an ethereal quality that aligns them with the color-field painters of the Abstract Expressionist group. On the other hand, the colors and shapes in Brooks's works on paper are more vibrant because the oils and gouaches do not run together as they do on canvas. The marks of the brush bristles are also more visible on paper and produce a surface that is highly textured and outwardly gestural.

Whereas Brooks's work on canvas and on paper prior to 1960 confronted the same issues of color, composition, and gesture, his paintings after 1960 are allover fields of color, while his drawings are composed almost exclusively of groups of black marks on broad open areas of white paper. He used black paint rather than ink, and after 1960, he used acrylic polymer rather than oil paint.[2] *Number 4—1960* (fig. 3) is one of a series of black-and-white works on paper created by Brooks during that year. It was executed in an acrylic polymer, which Brooks diluted with oil that, over time, unexpectedly produced stains around some of the edges of the painted areas. The work is composed of five black shapes in a simple open white field. Four were formed with a few broad brushstrokes and are dense and solid. Along their irregular borders are the unintended stains that create a golden halo effect. The fifth was made by rubbing a rather dry brush on the surface and then adding a curving black linear stroke at the left of this area. The result is an airy, fragmented, roughly elliptical shape whose sense of movement is further heightened by the sweeping stroke that accompanies it. The energy of the composition is enhanced by the varied directional motions of the five shapes—vertical, horizontal, and circular—and also by the interplay of positive and negative space created by these simple black forms on white paper. Other works in this series present similar shapes in more

3. *Number 4—1960*, 1960

complex, allover compositions, but in this one, each element stands out separately and boldly.

Neither the forms in Brooks's works nor his titles give any indication of specific subject matter. His organic shapes, suggestive of movement, growth, and decay, have prompted writers to associate them with nature. In 1986, one reviewer wrote that Brooks's works on paper evoke the impression of black marshland and white water.[3] The artist has denied such literal readings of his abstractions, but he has suggested that nature might enter into the work as an unconscious influence: "My paintings do not have their genesis in the contemplation of nature.... Nor do they end for me in imagery of that nature, although I would certainly not exclude the possibility of its being there. Too many people have seen it suggested there for me to ignore it."[4]

For Brooks, drawing was a parallel but secondary activity that enabled him to work out, on a smaller scale and in a quick and inexpensive fashion, the concerns in his paintings. He continued to work both on canvas and on paper until the mid-1980s. Because he was no longer physically capable of working on a large scale, Brooks stopped painting on canvas altogether in 1985, at the age of seventy-nine. Until his death in March of 1992, he worked exclusively on paper, continuing in the vein of earlier works such as *Number 4—1960* and persistently pursuing the Abstract Expressionist ideal to seek "the freedom of doing something more on impulse ... being irresponsible, in a sense ... using the medium in a new way, an accidental way, if possible."[5]

1. The possibility that Brooks's technique influenced other Abstract Expressionists has not been studied, but there is some evidence that Brooks may have inspired Pollock's 1951 series of ink drawings on rice paper. Brooks described his staining technique at a discussion among the Abstract Expressionist group that took place at Studio 35 in New York City in April 1950.

2. Brooks's shift to acrylic paint also occurred in his paintings after 1968. Acrylic paint was invented during the 1950s, and it became popular during the 1960s. Certain types are compatible with oil and others with water.

3. Vivian Raynor, "Art," *The New York Times,* June 20, 1986, p. C27.

4. James Brooks, quoted from Irving Sandler, "James Brooks and the Abstract Inscape," *Art News* 61 (February 1963), p. 63.

5. Brooks, quoted from April Kingsley, "James Brooks: Critique and Conversation," *Arts Magazine* 49, no. 8 (April 1975), p. 56.

Elaine de Kooning
1918*—1989

4. Untitled, Number 15, 1948
Enamel on paper, mounted on canvas
32 × 44 in. (81.3 × 111.8 cm)

Purchase, Iris Cantor Gift, 1992 (1992.22)

Elaine de Kooning was born in New York City in 1918. She had already attended art classes in New York, at the Leonardo da Vinci Art School in 1937 and at the American Artists School in 1938, when she first met Willem de Kooning in 1938. She was then twenty years old; he was fourteen years her senior and an accomplished artist. Shortly thereafter, she began to study with him, and they were married in 1943.

Despite her connections with the Abstract Expressionist group beginning in the early 1940s, Elaine de Kooning's work was never considered in this context until the recent discovery of seventeen previously unknown works in enamel on paper that she made in 1948. These pictures had been forgotten for about forty years before they were uncovered in Elaine de Kooning's basement. They reveal an artist at the beginning of her career exploring the same issues as her older Abstract Expressionist colleagues, and, seen as a series, they constitute a strong body of work that records her various approaches to the issues of gesturalism and figure-ground relationship. The best of them compare favorably with the work other Abstract Expressionists were creating from 1944 to 1948, notably William Baziotes, Arshile Gorky, and Willem de Kooning. Although her pictures clearly assimilate ideas already formulated by these older artists, de Kooning was able to make her own mark in the arena of early Abstract Expressionism. As Roberta Smith, in *The New York Times*, aptly wrote about these pictures, they add "more than a footnote, if less than a whole new chapter."[1]

Elaine de Kooning's earliest pictures were still lifes and cityscapes. In the early 1940s, when she began to paint self-portraits and interiors with figures, her subjects echoed those in Willem de Kooning's works of the same period. By 1947, her figures had become more abstract, and she began to experiment with biomorphic forms. In small, meticulously

13

drawn pencil studies of 1947, she created imagery that suggests the influence of Surrealist artists such as Salvador Dali, Max Ernst, Matta, and Yves Tanguy. Gorky, who was a close friend of Willem de Kooning's from 1930 until Gorky's death in 1948, was also influenced by Surrealism, and it is evident that in 1947, Elaine de Kooning was looking to Gorky's works as a source for her own.[2] She made shapes very similar to those in Gorky's pencil drawings of the mid-1940s, but she rendered them more three-dimensionally through her use of modeling and strong light-and-dark contrasts. In addition, whereas her forms are separated from one another by finely drawn borders, Gorky's are outlined but without much interior shading and are not concerned with neatness or finish. Over the next year, Elaine de Kooning's work began to correspond more closely to the gesturalism of Gorky, and of Willem de Kooning as well.

In the spring of 1948, the de Koonings faced a bleak financial future. In April–June, Willem had his first one-person exhibition at the Charles Egan Gallery in New York City, but he sold nothing. Elaine was earning a meager salary as an editorial associate for *Art News* magazine, writing art reviews for two dollars each.[3] Luckily, Willem received an invitation to teach from Josef Albers, director of the summer session at Black Mountain College in Asheville, North Carolina.[4] Offered room and board, two art studios, a small stipend, and round-trip transportation, the couple quickly accepted and arrived at Black Mountain in late June.

The de Koonings' summer was both enjoyable and productive, although Willem de Kooning later remarked: "The only thing wrong with the place is that if you are there, they want to give it to you."[5] This amusing criticism reflects a common belief among the Abstract Expressionist artists that poverty and struggle are necessary obstacles for the serious artist. Their financial problems made it necessary for these artists to be flexible in their uses of materials and, perhaps unwittingly, made them more open to experimentation with both materials and techniques. Elaine de Kooning explained: "There was a period in the first years of my marriage when all artists were extremely poor. Sometimes we did not even have the money to pay for materials. At times I would work on the back of a pad, which was all I had to paint on, or I would use wrapping paper, or take an old canvas that I really wasn't satisfied with and paint on that. However, I do not think of poverty as having been bad. It was good, as a sort of discipline."[6] Without money for canvas, Elaine de Kooning painted her 1948 series of seventeen abstractions on brown

4. Untitled, Number 15, 1948

wrapping paper, which she tacked to the wall of her small Black Mountain studio.[7]

In the smaller studies of this series, which measure about thirteen by sixteen inches, the artist seems constrained by size, especially when she attempted more loosely brushed compositions. In the larger works, she felt freer to more fully explore the qualities of gestural spontaneity and figure-ground relationship that she approached in some of the smaller ones. Untitled, Number 15 (fig. 4) is one of the largest pictures in this series; it is, in fact, the largest among the entire selection from the Museum's collection presented in this volume.

Throughout her Black Mountain series, Elaine de Kooning relied on an underlying grid structure to anchor her myriad forms and lines. In Untitled, Number 15, for example, vertical and horizontal bars are clearly defined as separate colored shapes, suggesting an architectural setting, perhaps windows or doors. This aspect of the composition relates to Stuart Davis's paintings of the late 1930s to early 1940s, such as *Swing Landscape* of 1938 and *Arboretum by Flashbulb* of 1942, which de Kooning saw several times at Davis's 1945 retrospective at the Museum of Modern Art. Impressed with his work, which she called "so clean-cut and without self-doubt,"[8] de Kooning wrote a twenty-page unpublished essay that is the basis for a much shorter article published in *Art News* in 1957.[9] A grid structure also exists in Willem de Kooning's *Asheville* and *Mailbox,* which he made at Black Mountain in the summer of 1948, although in both these paintings, the elaborately worked surfaces all but efface the underlying grid.

In Untitled, Number 15, several abstracted figures or parts of figures occupy the shallow space, along with various geometric configurations. Drips and spatters are incorporated, and showing through are the few areas of unpainted brown paper that escaped the artist's vigorous sweeping brushstrokes. Some elements overlap or push forward, but only slightly, so that the general impression is one of allover activity occurring on a single plane. All the elements are unified by the wide area of pink that flows throughout the entire composition. The unusual combinations of hot pinks, mustard yellows, greens, and blues in this picture are similar to colors in Willem de Kooning's work on paper of 1946 titled *Judgment Day* (see fig. 5), and to these, Elaine de Kooning has added large areas of beige and taupe. While in Willem de Kooning's picture, the mixture of oil paint over black charcoal produced a muted chalky texture, the shiny enamel used by Elaine de Kooning retains its glossy and intense color.

A year later, in 1949, Elaine de Kooning worked with greater linear abandon, although on a smaller scale, and she produced crayon abstractions on paper that relate to Jackson Pollock's allover works. Form and three-dimensional space are obscured, although there is a hint of a hidden figure beneath her web of slashing black lines. In 1950, Clement Greenberg and Meyer Schapiro selected Elaine de Kooning to be included in their "Talent 1950" exhibition at the Samuel Kootz Gallery. In 1952, the artist had her first one-person show at the Stable Gallery. Her social connections and her writings continued to place Elaine de Kooning in the context of Abstract Expressionist activities, but her work turned toward illustration and representation, albeit done with a gestural line, and it never again showed the dramatic intensity and daring of her brief Abstract Expressionist period during the late 1940s.

* Elaine de Kooning's birthdate was previously reported as 1920. A corrected date of 1918 was recently published in a chronology by the artist's sister Marjorie Luyckz, in Jane K. Bledsoe, *Elaine de Kooning*, exh. cat., Georgia Museum of Art, University of Georgia (Athens, Georgia, 1992).

1. Roberta Smith, "Art in Review," *The New York Times*, October 11, 1991, p. C28.

2. Four years later, the artist published a tribute to Gorky. See Elaine de Kooning, "Gorky: Painter of his own Legend," *Art News* 49 (January 1951), pp. 38–41, 63–66.

3. Elaine de Kooning would later gain prominence for her informative and astute features on contemporary artists for *Art News*.

4. Black Mountain College operated from 1933 to 1956 as a liberal-arts college, but in the summers, it became an innovative art colony that attracted guest teachers from various artistic fields. Its curriculum stressed the interrelationships among the arts, an idea that was based on the Bauhaus in Germany. The summer faculty in 1948 included John Cage for music, Merce Cunningham for dance, Richard Lippold and Peter Grippe for sculpture, Buckminster Fuller for architecture, Beaumont Newhall for photography, and Josef Albers and Willem de Kooning for painting. Elaine de Kooning attended various classes and participated in a theatrical production of Erik Satie's one-act comedy, *The Ruse of Medusa*, in which she played the role of Frisette.

5. Willem de Kooning, quoted from Martin Duberman, *Black Mountain: An Exploration in Community* (New York: E. P. Dutton, 1972), p. 283.

6. Elaine de Kooning, quoted from an unidentified article, Whitney Museum of American Art library, miscellaneous Elaine de Kooning file, p. 21.

7. These works were mounted on canvas much later. Other Abstract Expressionist painters, including Willem de Kooning, Franz Kline, and Mark Rothko, also created paintings on paper that were later mounted on canvas.

8. Elaine de Kooning, quoted from John Gruen, *The Party's Over Now* (New York: Viking Press, 1972), p. 214.

9. Elaine de Kooning, "Stuart Davis: True to Life," *Art News* 56 (April 1957), pp. 40–42, 54–55.

Willem de Kooning
Born 1904

5. *Judgment Day,* 1946
Oil and charcoal on paper
22⅛ × 28½ in. (56.2 × 72.4 cm)

From the Collection of Thomas B. Hess, jointly
owned by The Metropolitan Museum of Art and
the heirs of Thomas B. Hess, 1984 (1984.613.4)

6. Black Untitled, 1948
Oil and enamel on paper, mounted on
wood
29⅞ × 40¼ in. (75.9 × 102.2 cm)

From the Collection of Thomas B. Hess, jointly
owned by The Metropolitan Museum of Art and
the heirs of Thomas B. Hess, 1984 (1984.613.7)

7. Untitled, ca. 1949
Oil and enamel on paper
24⅛ × 20½ in. (61.3 × 52.1 cm)

Promised Gift of Muriel Kallis Newman,
The MURIEL KALLIS STEINBERG
NEWMAN Collection

8. *Zot,* 1949
Oil on paper, mounted on wood
18 × 20¼ in. (45.7 × 51.4 cm)

From the Collection of Thomas B. Hess, Purchase,
Rogers, Louis V. Bell and Harris Brisbane Dick
Funds and Joseph Pulitzer Bequest, and Gift of
the heirs of Thomas B. Hess, 1984 (1984.611)

9. *Woman,* 1950
Oil, cut and pasted paper on paper
14¾ × 11⅝ in. (37.5 × 29.5 cm)

From the Collection of Thomas B. Hess, jointly
owned by The Metropolitan Museum of Art and
the heirs of Thomas B. Hess, 1984 (1984.613.6)

5. *Judgment Day*, 1946

10. *Woman,* 1966
Oil on paper, mounted on cardboard
38 × 23¾ in. (96.5 × 60.3 cm)
Gift of Longview Foundation, Inc., in memory of
Audrey Stern Hess, 1975 (1975.189.6)

Willem de Kooning has been a masterful draftsman throughout his seventy-year-long career. His first known drawings were done in about 1921, while he was a young art student in Rotterdam. The few extant examples show that he displayed remarkable skill as a draftsman and was quite adept at realistic depiction of still-life objects using light and shade. De Kooning arrived in the United States in 1926, and during that year, he lived in Hoboken, New Jersey, where he worked as a housepainter. In 1927, he moved to New York City, and over the next few years, he developed acquaintances with other artists there that were of primary importance in his move from realism toward abstraction. Most notable are his friendships with John Graham from 1929 and with Arshile Gorky from the early 1930s. Graham was both a personal link with European art and a purveyor of mystical ideas through both his strange paintings of women and his book *System and Dialectics of Art.* Gorky was de Kooning's closest artistic compatriot during the evolutionary years of Abstract Expressionism; together, they visited the museums and discussed pictorial issues. De Kooning himself has acknowledged an enormous artistic debt to Gorky, with whom he remained close friends until Gorky's death in 1948.

During the years from 1934 to 1944, de Kooning was making both figurative works and abstractions composed of colored ovoids and rectangular shapes. During the 1930s, the figures were usually one or two men or women in an interior, and they demonstrate both de Kooning's technical abilities and a psychological dimension. In about 1940, de Kooning began to concentrate on images of women, a theme he was to develop continually throughout his career. During the early to mid-1940s, with the influence of Picasso and Surrealism in evidence, the two avenues of exploration he had followed over the past decade began to merge and further evolve in de Kooning's pictures.

In 1945–46, de Kooning created several complex compositions on both canvas and paper—*Pink Angels, Special*

6. Black Untitled, 1948

Delivery, and *Bill-Lee's Delight,*[1] for example—in which organic shapes, bloated and fragmented, exist in a labyrinth of darting black brushstrokes. One of the most intricate and colorful of this group is *Judgment Day* (fig. 5). Charcoal lines drawn over the dry painted surface, and sometimes also into the wet oil paint, define the colored shapes and create independent patterns as well. The high-pitched colors—acidic greens and yellows, vibrant oranges and pinks—are typical of de Kooning's work of the period. A geometric understructure of small and large rectangles corrals the larger biomorphs into four separate quadrants. As de Kooning noted, "even abstract shapes must have a likeness,"[2] and these forms suggest twisting fragmented body parts—torso, limbs, eyes, mouths—without being specifically human. In the center is a small white circle that stands out boldly and acts as a kind of pivotal point around which frenetic activity is occurring. Other circles and dots, evocative of disembodied eyes and mouths, are scattered around the composition.

De Kooning is one of Abstract Expressionism's most imaginative inventors of new forms, but his work is also informed by his knowledge of the ancient and contemporary art that he studied in museums and galleries. Picasso had a pervasive influence on early Abstract Expressionism, including de Kooning's art of the period, as the underlying structure and fragmented forms in *Judgment Day* demonstrate. De Kooning was a frequent visitor to The Metropolitan Museum of Art, and he was familiar with the ancient Roman frescoes from Boscoreale, the Old Master paintings, and Ingres's portraits. He was also an avid reader of the Metropolitan Museum's Bulletins, in which he could have seen examples of the prints of Pieter Brueghel. De Kooning's anthropomorphic beings bear a striking resemblance to Brueghel's bizarre creatures,[3] and although it is impossible to correlate any one source so directly with de Kooning's pictures, this is possibly among the many visual memories that enter into the work.

Shortly after completing *Judgment Day,* de Kooning was asked to create a backdrop for a dance recital being performed by Marie Marchowsky in New York City. According to Elaine de Kooning, the artist was paid only fifty dollars for the project, and "he didn't think for ten minutes about evolving a [new] composition for it. He blew up this painting with Milton Resnick in about three days with paint they bought for about $5.00 in a hardware store." *Judgment Day* "is the source of the backdrop, not a study for it," as has previously been thought.[4]

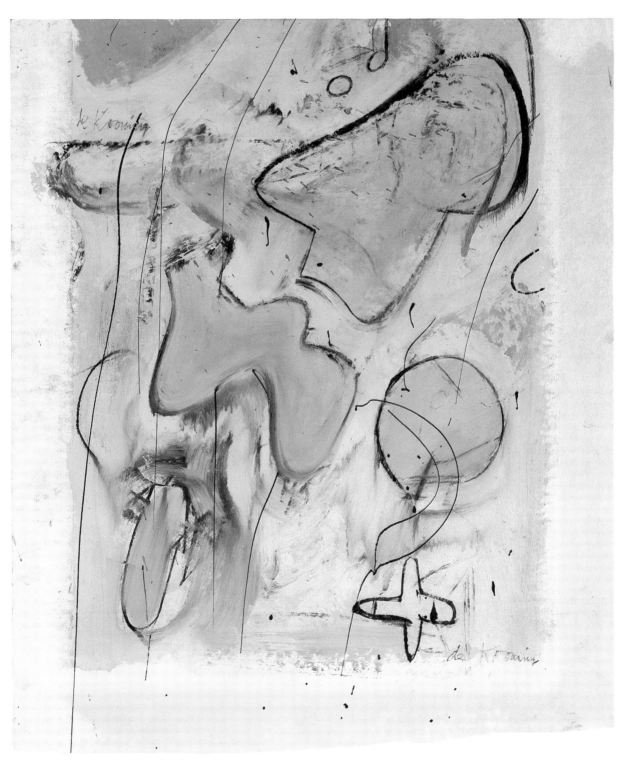

7. Untitled, ca. 1949

During the years from 1946 to 1949, de Kooning created a series of paintings on canvas and paper in which he continued his exploration of biomorphic abstraction, limiting himself primarily to black and white. Among that group are Black Untitled of 1948 (fig. 6), untitled of ca. 1949 (fig. 7), and *Zot* of 1949 (fig. 8). Like his friend Franz Kline, de Kooning used both black and white paint rather than letting the white of the paper show through. In untitled of ca. 1949, the whites vary from yellow to gray and from translucent to opaque. Black paint is used to outline a few larger shapes, which are surrounded by narrow drips of black paint. Elsewhere, smudges of yellow, rose, and turquoise show through the overall white wash. Although the forms in this piece are even more abstracted than the biomorphs in *Judgment Day,* they still evoke associations with imagery such as torso, head, star, moon, and sun. Black Untitled and *Zot* are allover compositions that display a more cohesive integration of positive and negative space. In Black Untitled, sweeping white rivers of paint rush across a black ground, creating writhing intertwining shapes that commingle figure and landscape references. A reclining figure, evocative of a deposed Christ, appears at the lower left.[5] While the black areas often resemble solid forms and the white marks linear interstices, these designations shift, and in some places, the black areas read as negative space around white mass. The composition suggests what Stephen Polcari has called "a continuity of things both organic and inorganic in a space both indoors and outdoors."[6]

In his small 1949 oil on paper titled *Zot,* as in several other pictures of the period, de Kooning began the composition by drawing random letters on the surface. As de Kooning progressed with his series of black-and-white pictures, white became the dominant color, and black was used to create the calligraphic accents that outline shapes. This group of pictures culminated in 1949 with de Kooning's masterful painting *Attic,*[7] in which every element coheres to communicate what the artist has called a "no-environment," an indefinable place that could be an interior or an exterior, a figure or nature. In *Attic,* de Kooning fully realized his intention to use opposing elements to evoke an anxious balance that can be glimpsed only momentarily.

In the works that followed *Zot* and *Attic,* de Kooning resumed his use of color as he began making the series for

8. *Zot*, 1949

which he is best known, the Women. The Museum's *Woman* of 1950 (fig. 9) is a splendid example of this subject. This painting on paper is one of the most lively and fully realized of de Kooning's small-scale Women. A wide-eyed young woman with flaming red hair and a congenial lipsticked smile stares out at the viewer. Her head and eyes, which are incised into the wet paint with a pencil point, are among the few body parts that are clearly delineated. Outlined with black paint are an arm with stick fingers, a calf and thigh, and a pair of eyelike breasts. The rest of the figure merges into its setting in a jumble of slashing brushstrokes of bright primary and secondary colors. Small patches of blue, green, orange, yellow, and red peek out from beneath the off-white strokes of paint that further camouflage the image. The work is fraught with the palpable tensions, as well as the humor, that enliven de Kooning's 1950 to 1953 series of large-scale Woman paintings. It is one of many small drawings and oils on paper de Kooning produced concurrently that contributed to the evolution of this theme. Although this picture does not resemble the 1950–52 final version of *Woman I,* which is in the collection of the Museum of Modern Art in New York, the small figure's features and pose correlate to two late stages in the process of painting *Woman I* that occurred at the end of 1951 and were subsequently painted over. Other similarities to pencil drawings of 1951–52 support the possibility that this *Woman* may have been executed a year or two later than is presently reported.

In the large-scale Woman paintings, and in other works on paper from the 1950s, de Kooning incorporated collage elements into the composition as a point of departure. Here, as in *Woman I,* a bright red mouth was cut out from a magazine cigarette ad and pasted on the support. De Kooning alluded to its significance: "First of all I felt everything ought to have a mouth. Maybe it was like a pun, maybe it's even sexual . . . it helped me immensely to have this real thing. I don't know why I did it with the mouth. Maybe the grin —it's rather like the Mesopotamian idols."[8] This reference to Mesopotamian idols has recently been associated with two Sumerian statues in the Metropolitan Museum's collection that were on exhibit during the 1940s and 1950s.[9] De Kooning has noted the connection between his Women and the paintings of women through the ages, and such broader correlations and the emotions they stimulate for de Kooning were set forth by the artist in 1951: "Spiritually I am whatever my

9. *Woman*, 1950

spirit allows me to be, and that is not necessarily in the future. I have no nostalgia, however. If I am confronted with one of those small Mesopotamian figures, I have no nostalgia for it, but, instead, I may get into a state of anxiety. Art never seems to me peaceful or pure. I always seem to be wrapped in the melodrama of vulgarity. I do not think of inside or outside—or of art in general—as a situation of comfort."[10]

The seemingly random gesturalism and the open-ended quality of this picture exemplify de Kooning's rejection of the traditional criteria of "finish," a characteristically held Abstract Expressionist idea that relates to the process of painting as self-discovery. In a 1948 roundtable discussion at Studio 35 in New York, de Kooning said: "I refrain from 'finishing' it. I paint myself out of the picture. . . . There seems to be a time when I lose sight of what I wanted to do, and then I am out of it. If the picture has a countenance, I keep it. If it hasn't, I throw it away. I am not really very much interested in the question."[11]

By 1955, de Kooning was no longer using black outlines to distinguish the contours of his figures. Broad slashes of color now encroached more and more into the domain of the figure, resulting in a further fusion of figure and landscape.[12] From about 1955 until 1963, de Kooning eliminated the human figure from his compositions, and produced very abstract pictures with greatly simplified shapes and colors that alluded to both urban and rural landscapes. Very few drawings were produced between 1960 and 1963, during which time the artist was engaged in building a studio on Long Island. It has been suggested that "this hiatus provided a period of gestation in which the older images could be incorporated into the paintings."[13]

De Kooning's permanent move to The Springs, East Hampton, Long Island, in June of 1963 brought a new vitality and light to his paintings and a reappearance of the Women—voluptuous women with creamy pink skin and bright red lips. In his 1966 oil on paper *Woman* (fig. 10), one of these nubile muses coyly turns to face the viewer in midstride, her face partially hidden by long blond hair and a raised arm. She is a step beyond the earlier Women and seems to grow directly out of the painterly gesture. The spontaneous muscular brushstrokes create quivering swirls of sensuous thick paint that characterize de Kooning's mature work and epitomize his 1951 statement: "Flesh is the reason why oil painting was invented."[14]

10. *Woman*, 1966

1. *Pink Angels,* ca. 1945, oil and charcoal on canvas, 52 × 40 in., Collection the Weisman Family; *Special Delivery,* 1946, oil, enamel, and charcoal on cardboard, 23⅛ × 30 in., Collection Hirshhorn Museum and Sculpture Garden, Smithsonian Institution, Washington, D.C.; *Bill-Lee's Delight,* 1946, oil on paper, mounted on composition board, 27½ × 34½ in., Collection Mr. and Mrs. Lee V. Eastman.

2. Willem de Kooning, quoted from Thomas B. Hess, *Willem de Kooning* (New York: The Museum of Modern Art, 1968), p. 47.

3. Willem de Kooning told William S. Lieberman that he read the Museum's Bulletins; reproductions of prints by Brueghel appeared in the June 1943 issue. In Sally Yard, *Willem de Kooning: The First Twenty-Six Years in New York* (New York: Garland Publishing, 1986), p. 146, it is suggested that *Judgment Day* "portrays the four angels of the *Gates of Paradise* and was influenced by the Boscoreale frescoes at the Metropolitan Museum."

4. Elaine de Kooning, quoted from "Artist Questionnaire," September 9, 1988, on file in Department of 20th Century Art archives, The Metropolitan Museum of Art, New York.

5. In ca. 1949–50, de Kooning made a smaller related black enamel untitled drawing on paper, measuring 21 × 29 in., which is in the collection of Mr. and Mrs. Ralph I. Goldenberg.

6. Stephen Polcari, *Abstract Expressionism and the Modern Experience* (Cambridge: Cambridge University Press, 1991), p. 280.

7. *Attic,* 1949 oil, enamel, and newspaper transfer on canvas, 61⅞ × 81 in., jointly owned by The Metropolitan Museum of Art and Muriel Kallis Newman, in honor of her son Glenn David Steinberg, The MURIEL KALLIS STEINBERG NEWMAN Collection, 1982 (1982.16.3).

8. Willem de Kooning, quoted from Diane Waldman, *Willem de Kooning in East Hampton*, exh. cat., The Solomon R. Guggenheim Museum (New York, 1978), p. 22.

9. See Yard, p. 188.

10. Willem de Kooning, quoted from "What Abstract Art Means to Me," *Bulletin of the Museum of Modern Art* 18, no. 3 (Spring 1951).

11. Willem de Kooning, quoted from "Artists' Sessions at Studio 35," April 1950, in Robert Motherwell and Ad Reinhardt, eds., *Modern Artists in America* (New York: Wittenborn Schultz, 1952), p. 12.

12. A connection between de Kooning's work after 1950 and Chaim Soutine has been suggested in the following three works: Irving Sandler, *The Triumph of American Painting* (New York: Harper & Row Publishers, 1978), p. 130; William C. Seitz, *Abstract Expressionist Painting in America* (Cambridge, Mass.: Harvard University Press, 1983), p. 78; and Yard, p. 187. The Museum of Modern Art in New York held a Soutine retrospective from October 1950 to January 1951.

13. Paul Cummings, "The Drawings of Willem de Kooning," *Willem de Kooning: Drawings, Paintings, Sculpture*, exh. cat., Whitney Museum of American Art (New York, 1983), p. 20.

14. Willem de Kooning, quoted from a statement titled "The Renaissance and Order," 1950; reprinted in Hess, p. 142.

Arshile Gorky
1904–1948

11. *Virginia Landscape,* 1943
Pencil and colored crayons on paper
17 × 22 in. (43.2 × 55.9 cm)

Promised Gift of Muriel Kallis Newman,
The MURIEL KALLIS STEINBERG
NEWMAN Collection

12. Untitled, 1944
Graphite and colored crayons on paper
18 × 24 in. (45.7 × 61 cm)

Promised Gift of Muriel Kallis Newman,
The MURIEL KALLIS STEINBERG
NEWMAN Collection

Arshile Gorky has been considered the last Surrealist, the first Abstract Expressionist, and, more recently, a transitional figure. Although he was friendly with and exhibited with artists from both groups, Gorky did not consider himself a member of either. His melancholy nostalgia for his homeland of Armenia, which he left at age sixteen, gave him a sense of separateness from these circles of European and American artists. Nevertheless, Gorky's work of the 1940s has the same confluence of ideas that is evident in the contemporaneous work of William Baziotes, Gerome Kamrowski, Richard Pousette-Dart, and Mark Rothko. However, because Gorky died in 1948, at a critical juncture in Abstract Expressionist art when radical changes were taking place, his work can be related only to the earlier stages of the new American painting.

In 1920, Gorky arrived in the United States and began taking art lessons in Massachusetts and in Rhode Island. He moved to New York City in late 1924, and in 1925, he enrolled at the Grand Central School of Art, where he eventually taught until 1931. During the mid- to late 1920s, Gorky painted still lifes and landscapes that reflect the influence of Paul Cézanne. By the 1930s, he was creating pictures with flat interlocking colored shapes that reflected his interest in

Synthetic Cubism, particularly in the work of Picasso. His involvement with Cubism was reinforced by his friendship with the artists Stuart Davis and John Graham. Gorky met some of the Abstract Expressionists when he was painting murals for the Works Progress Administration during the 1930s. His closest friend among those artists was Willem de Kooning, whom he met in 1933 and with whom he shared a studio in New York City for several years. This friendship, of great mutual benefit both artistically and personally, continued until Gorky's death in 1948. The biomorphic images that de Kooning made during the mid- to late 1940s, as well as those done by Elaine de Kooning in 1948, show the influence exerted by Gorky, and, indeed, Willem de Kooning has frequently acknowledged this debt.

Gorky's work took a new direction in 1942, when his biomorphic shapes became linear notations, existing independently from the colored areas in the pictures and empowered with a range of associative meanings. In February of 1942, Gorky wrote to his sister Vartoosh: "Loving memories of our garden in Armenia's Khorkom haunt me frequently. . . . In my art I often draw our garden and recreate its precious greenery and life."[1] That summer, Gorky spent three weeks in New Milford, Connecticut, where he worked directly from nature, using it as a medium through which he could recall childhood experiences. He also equated nature with the themes of fertility and regeneration, which were in part a reflection on his marriage to Agnes Magruder in September of 1941 and the couple's hopes for a family. In his February 1942 letter to Vartoosh, Gorky also wrote: "The stuff of thought is the seed of the artist. And as the eye functions as the brain's sentry, I communicate my most private perceptions through art, my view of the world. In trying to probe beyond the ordinary, and the unknown, I create an inner infinity."[2] In this early statement of his intentions, Gorky directly aligns himself with the Abstract Expressionist idea of beginning with personal experience to express universal truths.[3]

During the years 1943 and 1944, Gorky spent many productive months at his in-laws' country estate, called Crooked Hill Farm, near Hamilton, Virginia. The rolling hills, open grazing fields, and wooded thickets reminded him of Armenia. He drew in the fields, looking both into the grass and toward the distant panoramas. With sheets of paper tacked to a drawing board or bound in a notebook for easy mobility, he drew mostly with pencils and wax crayons. He sharpened his pencils with a knife to an inch-long point, and de

11. *Virginia Landscape*, 1943

Kooning remembered in 1971 that Gorky spoke of using pencils "like a surgeon's tool."[4] He drew *Virginia Landscape* (fig. 11) while at the farm for three months during the summer of 1943, and he made the untitled drawing shown here (fig. 12) during a nine-month stay there the following year. Gorky's forays into nature during 1943 and 1944 resulted in hundreds of drawings, and many were sources for his paintings, although neither of the two drawings in this selection has been related to a specific painting.

In *Virginia Landscape*, Gorky's pencil line is richly varied, ranging from delicate fine lines to vigorously rubbed strokes. A few of the shapes are partially shaded with pencil, especially at the pointed tips, but there is little or no sense of three-dimensionality.[5] Scattered around the sheet are roughly circular and elliptical smudges of bright color—red, blue, green, yellow—drawn with wax crayons. In December of 1944, Gorky wrote to Vartoosh of "capturing the homeland's colors . . . the rich colors of our fruits. Apricots, peaches, apples, grapes. The rich colors of our plants and vegetation, our grains and flowers. Always I try to duplicate the colors of Armenia in my works."[6] Sometimes these colors stay within the borders of a particular shape, but at other times, they are totally independent of the penciled lines. Their waxy surfaces have been rubbed, scraped, and erased to produce veils of color similar to those in Gorky's paintings of the period that were made with diluted oil paint, such as the Metropolitan Museum's *Water of the Flowery Mill* of 1944. The wealth of biomorphic imagery is somehow familiar but not exactly recognizable. Images suggest human figures, flowers, and birds. Dreams, memories, and observations of things seen coalesce to produce what André Breton, in 1945, called "hybrid forms in which all human emotion is precipitated."[7]

In Gorky's untitled drawing of 1944 (fig. 12), the sensuously rounded biomorphism of *Virginia Landscape* has been pulled taut into more squared-off shapes and sharp, straighter lines, and color has all but disappeared into a few narrow streaks of red, yellow, and green. A comparison of these two drawings clearly demonstrates Gorky's ability to manipulate line for varied expressive purposes and to elevate line to a primary element in his work. During the years 1944 to 1947, line was the most important feature in Gorky's paintings on canvas, although the fluidly painted lines rarely match the intense agitation evoked by the pencil marks.

The importance of drawing for Gorky is exemplified in a letter written in about 1948–49 by his wife, Agnes Magruder, in which she noted: "When he painted from his drawings it

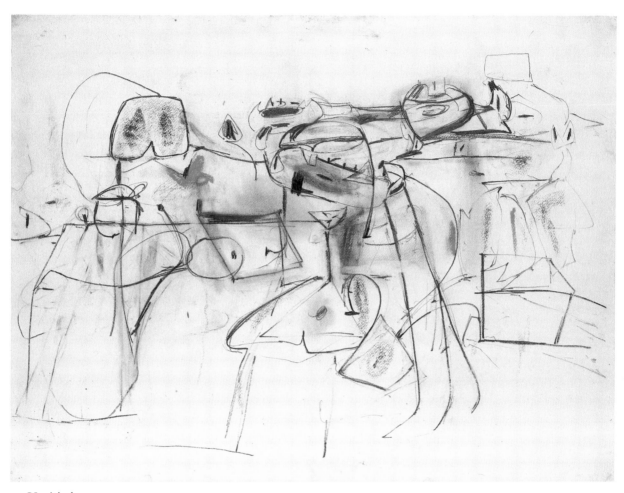

12. Untitled, 1944

was different from drawing from nature because he was editing his own emotion and adding and using all his conscious knowledge of his art. This produced some wonderful paintings, but he sometimes said he wished he could . . . make the paintings as direct on the canvas as the emotion was within him in front of nature"[8] when he was drawing.

1. Arshile Gorky, quoted from a letter to Vartoosh Mooradian, February 9, 1942; reprinted in *Ararat* (Fall 1971), pp. 28–29.

2. Ibid., p. 29.

3. Some writers, Harry Rand, for example, have sought to provide exact interpretations for Gorky's imagery, but the specificity of such readings misses Gorky's intention to engender multiple references both in his own mind and in the viewer's mind.

4. Willem de Kooning, "Remembrances of Gorky," *Ararat* (Fall 1971), p. 50.

5. The precise linearity in Gorky's drawings also appears after 1945 in many of his paintings, in which thin black lines are drawn in paint with a commercial liner brush used by sign painters.

6. Gorky, quoted from a letter to Vartoosh Mooradian, December 1944; reprinted in *Ararat* (Fall 1971), p. 33.

7. André Breton, "The Eyespring—Arshile Gorky," *Arshile Gorky*, trans. Julien Levy (New York: Julien Levy Gallery, 1945).

8. Agnes Magruder, quoted from a letter to Ethel Schwabacher, Arshile Gorky file, Whitney Museum of American Art, New York, ca. 1948–49; reprinted in Diane Waldman, *Arshile Gorky 1904–1948: A Retrospective*, exh. cat., The Solomon R. Guggenheim Museum (New York: Harry N. Abrams, 1981), p. 57.

Adolph Gottlieb
1903–1974

13. *Signs for Magic,* 1946
Gouache on paper
15⅜ × 11¼ in. (39.1 × 28.6 cm)
Gift of Mr. and Mrs. Arthur Wiesenberger, 1967
(67.225)

In 1941, Adolph Gottlieb and Mark Rothko, who had been Gottlieb's close friend since about 1930, saw a correlation between the anxiety fostered by the onset of World War II and ancient people's "recognition and acceptance of the brutality of the natural world as well as the eternal insecurity of life."[1] They believed that art should reflect contemporary humanity's link with the past, and their aim was to create universal symbols that could express this continuity. Primitive art and ancient mythology provided the starting point, coupled with elements from both Cubism and Surrealism as well as ideas set forth in philosophy, psychology, and literature. That same year, Gottlieb began making works he called pictographs.

The word "pictograph" alludes to prehistoric paintings on rock. The format of Gottlieb's pictographs is an irregular grid; within each area, one or more simplified images or abstract signs appear—heads, eyes, handprints, geometric shapes, and a variety of linear configurations, for example, recur often. These works are in part an outgrowth of Gottlieb's earlier pictures, particularly those he made in 1938 in Arizona in which various desert objects, painted realistically and juxtaposed in boxlike compartments, create a surreal atmosphere. In 1967, Gottlieb said of his pictographs: "I would start by having an arbitrary division of the canvas into roughly rectangular areas, and with the process of free association I would put various images and symbols within these compartments. . . . There was no logical or rational design in the placing of these . . . then when all of these images and symbols were combined, they could not be read like a rebus. There was no direct connection one to the other . . . by the strange juxtapositions that occurred, a new kind of significance occurred, a new kind of significance stemmed from this juxtaposition."[2]

Gottlieb's statement reiterates the importance of creating a new kind of subject matter, an issue held in common by the Abstract Expressionists. Gottlieb, with Rothko and Barnett Newman, authored the first official declaration in this regard in a now-famous letter published in *The New York Times* in June of 1943.[3] In 1947, Gottlieb spoke more specifically about the meaning underlying his pictographs and its significance for the contemporary world: "The role of the artist, of course, has always been that of image maker. Different times require different images. Today, when our aspirations have been reduced to a desperate attempt to escape from evil and times are out of joint, our obsessive, subterranean, and pictographic images are the expression of the neurosis which is our reality. To my mind, certain so-called abstraction is not abstraction at all. On the contrary, it is the realism of our time."[4]

Signs for Magic (fig. 13) is a small gouache on paper made by Gottlieb in 1946 in his Brooklyn Heights studio. It is one of many pictographs he made on paper, none of which is a study for a painting. The imagery in this composition includes disembodied eyes, a head in profile, an outstretched arm and four-fingered hand, and many more cryptic shapes. Several of the elements reappear frequently over the years in the pictographs, always varied in color and execution and in their placement in the overall format. The critic Lawrence Alloway noted that whenever Gottlieb "happened to learn of preexisting meanings attached to any of his pictographs, they became unusable. The signs needed to be evocative, but unassigned."[5] The ghostly white gun is the most representational image in this work; its appearance is particularly unsettling and seems to confirm Gottlieb's intention to make his pictographs relevant to contemporary society.

In 1950, Gottlieb noted of himself and his fellow Abstract Expressionists: "It is a mistaken assumption that any departure from tradition stems from ignorance...[it]... is a problem of knowing what that tradition is and being willing to reject it in part. This requires familiarity with the past. I think that we have this familiarity, and if we depart from tradition, it is out of knowledge, not innocence."[6] Evident in *Signs for Magic,* as in all Gottlieb's pictographs, is his knowledge of African and American Indian art, as well as of Cubism and Surrealism. Eyes and abstract symbols such as the ones here appear frequently in Joan Miró and Paul Klee, for example, and the head in profile and the eyes resemble

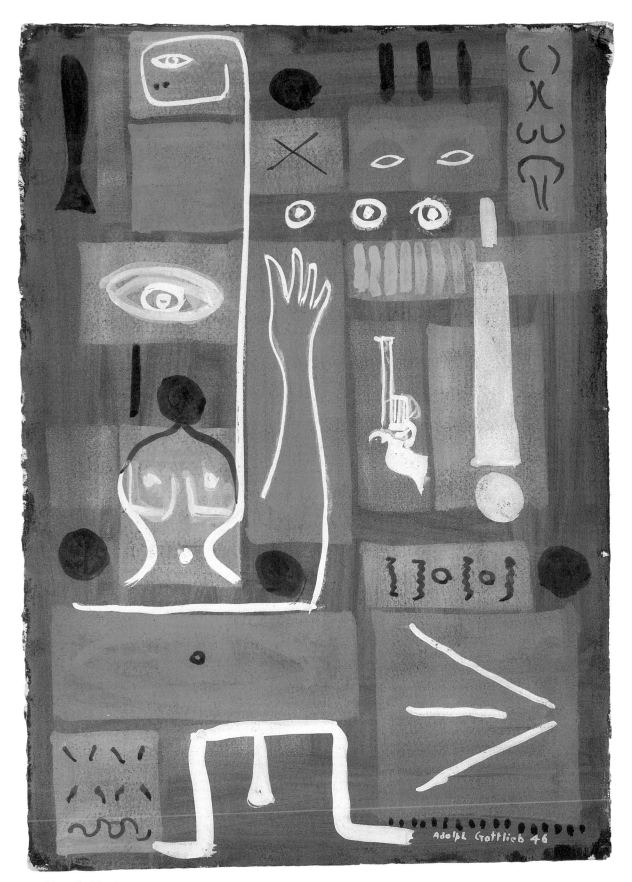

13. *Signs for Magic,* 1946

forms in Picasso's works of the 1920s and 1930s.[7] The palette of browns, ochers, oranges, whites, and blacks is close to that of early Cubism; in this pictograph, it enhances the direct sense of the primitive that Gottlieb sought. The irregular grid is a Cubist-derived structure, but it is used by Gottlieb to achieve a very different objective. As the artist said of his pictographs, "There was no beginning, and no end, no definite focal point."[8]

In *Signs for Magic,* Gottlieb painted about sixteen separate rectangles of varying size and color—white, ocher, and orange—over a brown-black ground. Depending on their color, the rectangles advance or recede slightly in the shallow space. Over them, Gottlieb drew the individual images with black, white, or orange gouache. This format differs somewhat from his characteristic method of dividing the space with vertical and horizontal lines. In addition, unlike many of the other pictographs, in which the images are completely contained within the confines of one area, some images here extend over several rectangles. This variation demonstrates that, in about 1946, as Harry Rand has noted, "Gottlieb was by no means certain about the direction his work was going in at the time. In some works the grid predominates, in others the signs appear the foremost element."[9] Free association, chance discovery, and change are all part of Gottlieb's creative process, and they are evident in his method of reworking the surfaces of both his oil paintings and his works on paper. In the canvases, the paint is often thickly layered, as images are made and then covered over. In the gouaches on paper, such as *Signs for Magic,* there is a similar layering, but here the medium's translucency allows us to see the rectangles from previous layers.

Gottlieb continued to produce his pictographs until 1953, and their representational imagery differed from the more abstract images being produced by the other Abstract Expressionists at that time. However, by 1951–53, a further shift in Gottlieb's work was occurring; his forms became more abstract and fewer in number. In 1957, Gottlieb began his last series; they are called "Bursts" and are characteristically composed of one or more orbs above a jagged, gesturally painted area. At about that time, he is reported to have said: "Abstraction is not a limitation but a liberation."[10] Gottlieb continued to confront the same issues in the "Bursts" that he had faced in his pictographs. Like his fellow Abstract Expressionists, he expanded the size and simplified the imagery to express his subject matter in more abstract universal terms.

1. Adolph Gottlieb and Mark Rothko, quoted from "The Portrait and the Modern Artist," broadcast on "Art in New York," WNYC Radio, October 13, 1943; transcript in Adolph and Esther Gottlieb Foundation Archives, New York City.

2. Gottlieb, quoted from an interview with Jeanne Siegel, WBAI Radio, May 1967, New York; transcript in Museum of Modern Art Library.

3. For this letter in full, see Clifford Ross, ed., *Abstract Expressionism: Creators and Critics—An Anthology* (New York: Harry N. Abrams, 1990), pp. 205–7.

4. Gottlieb, quoted from "The Ides of Art," *Tiger's Eye* 1, no. 2 (December 1947), p. 43.

5. Lawrence Alloway, "Melpomene and Graffiti," *Art International* 12 (April 1968), pp. 21–22.

6. Gottlieb, quoted from "Artists' Sessions at Studio 35," 1950; published in Robert Motherwell and Ad Reinhardt, eds., *Modern Artists in America* (New York: Wittenborn Schultz, 1952), p. 13.

7. There is a similarity between *Signs for Magic* and Picasso's pair of paintings, both titled *Three Musicians* and both of 1921, one in the collection of The Museum of Modern Art in New York and the other in the Philadelphia Museum of Art, which were illustrated in The Museum of Modern Art's *Picasso: Fifty Years of his Art*, published in 1946, the same year Gottlieb made *Signs for Magic*.

8. Gottlieb, interview with Siegel.

9. Harry Rand, "Adolph Gottlieb in Context," *Arts* 51, no. 6 (February 1977), p. 120.

10. Gottlieb, quoted from Selden Rodman, *Conversations with Artists* (New York: Devin-Adair Co., 1957), p. 89.

Philip Guston
1913–1980

14. Untitled, ca. 1950–51
Pen and ink on paper
18 × 23⅛ in. (45.7 × 58.7 cm)
Promised Gift of Muriel Kallis Newman,
The MURIEL KALLIS STEINBERG
NEWMAN Collection

15. *Drawing 1960,* 1960
Pen and ink on paper
17⅞ × 24 in. (45.4 × 61 cm)
Rogers Fund, 1973 (1973.13)

In 1973, Philip Guston stated: "It is the bareness of drawing that I like. The act of drawing is what locates, suggests, discovers. At times it seems enough to draw, without the distractions of color and mass. . . . Usually, I draw in relation to my painting, what I am working on at the time. On a lucky day a surprising balance of forms and spaces will appear and I feel the drawing making itself, the image taking hold. This in turn moves me towards painting—anxious to get to the same place, with the actuality of paint and light."[1]

Although Guston's main focus was always painting, over the course of his fifty-year-long career, he frequently turned to drawing. He produced works on paper in cycles that could extend over several years, as if he had to assimilate changes in his artistic direction first on paper before applying them to his large paintings on canvas. Such drawings often marked a transition in his work. As one writer said in 1988, drawing was Guston's "problem-solving" medium; it helped him "work out new formal and pictorial solutions."[2] Often, an intense period of drawing was followed by a lengthy time of working exclusively on paintings. Although the drawings were made in series, their compositions relate to one another only in a general way; they are not variations of the same image. Few of them are preliminary sketches for specific paintings.

14. Untitled, ca. 1950–51

Between 1950 and 1954, Guston created a remarkable group of black-on-white drawings, in which he achieved great diversity by variously placing and combining abstract marks on an empty white space. As Dore Ashton noted in 1976, Guston reduced forms "to their most elemental signs. He constrained them, turned them, made them rush like torrents on the white of the page, or form arabesques flowing into nowhere at the edges."[3]

Like all the works in this group, untitled of ca. 1950–51 (fig. 14) is drawn with black ink and a quill pen, whose graphic versatility is displayed in this sheet. Short thick strokes mass together at various points, and, in contrast, thinner wavering marks trail off into broken double lines. The marks gather at the center and dart back and forth in broken yet fluid rhythms. Thick and thin, light and dark, inward toward the center and outward from it, the motions convey the obsessive manner in which Guston worked, yet they are regulated by the artist's control of his pen and by the amount of pressure and ink used in the execution. In 1978, Guston related his method to that of Chinese painting: "Sung period training involves doing something thousands and thousands of times—bamboo shoots and birds—until someone else does it, not you, and the rhythm moves through you. I think that is what the Zen Buddhists called 'satori' and I have had it happen to me. It is a double activity, when you know and you don't know, and it shouldn't really be talked about. So I move toward that moment."[4]

Guston was seeking to create an allover imagery composed of multiple parts that would read as a single entity. To this end, he used as an example Piet Mondrian's "plus-and-minus" pictures of the 1910s, such as the *Pier and Ocean* and *Church Facade* series.[5] Guston's marks, however, strain against the strictly vertical and horizontal orientation that Mondrian used. In this drawing, as in several others, there are curves and arcs that evoke organic energy. These works differ, however, from Jackson Pollock's allover compositions. Guston's marks are not spread out evenly over the entire surface; instead, they are concentrated at the center. A relationship of figure and ground still exists here, and it is in his paintings of 1951–54 that Guston more thoroughly integrated these two elements.

Guston's paintings and drawings of 1950–51 brought him recognition as an Abstract Expressionist. Guston was absent from the New York art world from 1940 until 1950, when he settled permanently in New York City. He and Pollock had

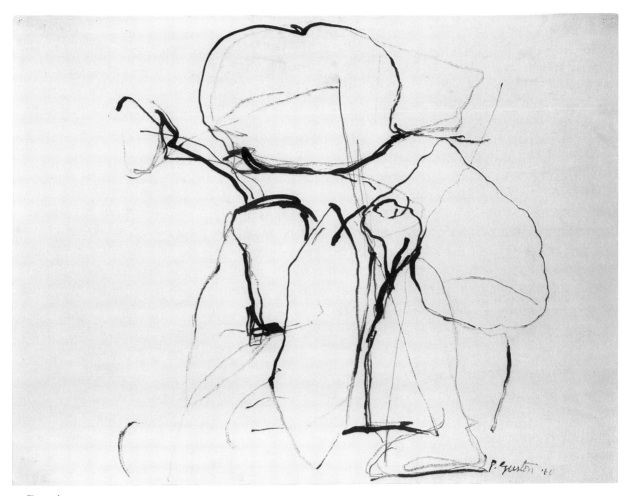

15. *Drawing 1960*, 1960

been old friends since they were in high school together from 1927 to 1929. Guston met other Abstract Expressionists —Adolph Gottlieb, Willem de Kooning, and Mark Rothko— during the mid-1930s, when he was living in New York and working for the Works Progress Administration. He had been a close friend of Bradley Walker Tomlin, who had been a neighbor in Woodstock, New York, since 1947. Yet, despite these associations, it was not until 1950 that Guston made abstract works that could be related to those of these Abstract Expressionists, who had already spent several years developing their mature signature work. Just two years prior to his artistic transformation, Guston was producing fairly representational narratives. His transition to gestural abstraction is apparent in the series of pen-and-ink drawings he made in 1948–49, during his travels through Europe while on a Prix de Rome and a grant from the American Academy of Arts and Letters. In these sketches, Guston captured the linear structure of the architectural sites and the streets, using delicate spidery vertical and horizontal lines to create images that are almost completely abstract. The strong similarity between these drawings and Guston's drawings of the early 1950s suggests that, even at its most abstract, his art never relinquished its tie to figuration, and, indeed, by the 1960s, he had begun to move again in that direction.

Drawing 1960 (fig. 15) exemplifies the series of drawings Guston produced during the early to mid-1960s. His works from the 1960s and later often relate to his paintings and drawings from the 1940s, and this series resembles his 1947–48 painting titled *Tormentors* and the pen-and-ink sketches that preceded it, in which both representational and more abstracted linear passages appear. Eliminating the narrative references, Guston isolated those sections of the early drawing in which line existed as an abstract element. Enlarged on an off-white sheet of paper in *Drawing 1960*, these passages became nervously outlined shapes that suggest tangible forms without being specifically descriptive. About this time, Guston remarked: "The trouble with recognizable art is that it excludes too much. I want my work to include more. . . . I am therefore driven to scrape out the recognition, to efface it, to erase it. I am nowhere until I have reduced it to semi-recognition."[6] There is a marked similarity between the bean-shaped form at the top of *Drawing 1960* and the wide-eyed disembodied heads that haunt Guston's pictures of the 1970s.

In *Drawing 1960*, irregular shapes confront one another in a shallow space. Most of them are pushed together and overlap slightly in the bottom half of the composition, with the bean shape above them. Wavy lines enmesh the whole in a tight, centrally located bundle. As in his untitled drawing of ca. 1950–51, Guston manipulates pen and ink to achieve a range of tones and textures, from heavier dark opaque black marks to thinner dry mottled gray lines that seem in danger of disintegrating. As he progressed in this series, Guston isolated fewer shapes at the center of the blank white page and did not join them with linear tethers. In a state of "semirecognition," these shapes began to describe the recurrent forms that would soon characterize Guston's late work.

1. Philip Guston, quoted from David Aronson, "Philip Guston: Ten Drawings," *Boston University Journal* (Fall 1973), p. 21; reprinted in Magdalena Dabrowski, *The Drawings of Philip Guston* (New York: Museum of Modern Art, 1988), p. 9.

2. Dabrowski, p. 10.

3. Dore Ashton, *Yes, but . . . : A Critical Study of Philip Guston* (New York: Viking Press, 1976), p. 97.

4. Guston, quoted from a 1978 statement; reprinted in Dore Ashton, ed., *Twentieth-Century Artists on Art* (New York: Pantheon Books, 1985), p. 212.

5. For more information, see Dabrowski, pp. 24–25.

6. Guston, quoted from "Philip Guston's Object: A Dialogue with Harold Rosenberg"; reprinted in Sam Hunter, *Philip Guston: Recent Paintings and Drawings*, exh. cat., The Jewish Museum (New York, 1966).

Gerome Kamrowski
Born 1914

16. *Revolve and Devolve,* 1943
Gouache on paper
20 × 29¾ in. (50.8 × 75.6 cm)
Purchase, Anna-Maria and Stephen Kellen
Foundation and Mrs. Fernand Leval Gifts, 1988
(1988.214)

17. *Forest Forms,* 1943
Gouache, crayon, brush and ink on paper
22 × 29⅞ in. (55.9 × 75.9 cm)
Purchase, Lila Acheson Wallace Gift, 1990 (1990.13.1)

Gerome Kamrowski arrived in New York City in 1938, when he was twenty-four years old. His work that year featured planar constructions and geometric abstractions characteristic of the New Bauhaus in Chicago and the Hans Hofmann School in Provincetown, Massachusetts, both of which he had recently attended. These nonobjective pictures earned Kamrowski a stipend for nearly a decade from Baroness Hilla Rebay, Director of Solomon Guggenheim's Museum of Non-Objective Painting in New York. The money allowed him to live in New York, where he became involved with a group of artists who were experimenting with Surrealist ideas and techniques, which, ironically, were abhorrent to Rebay. By the mid-1930s, while he was living in Minnesota, Kamrowski had developed an intellectual curiosity about Surrealism through his reading of magazines such as *Minotaure* and *Transition* and also through traveling exhibitions such as the Museum of Modern Art's *Fantastic Art, Dada, and Surrealism* of 1936–37. These ideas did not affect his art until 1939, when he became friendly with New York artists such as William Baziotes, Jimmy Ernst (son of the Surrealist Max Ernst), Matta, and Jackson Pollock. Within only months after his move to New York, Kamrowski's art underwent a transformation from geometric to biomorphic abstraction.

By 1943, the date of the two drawings shown here, Kamrowski had assimilated a number of influences. *Revolve*

16. *Revolve and Devolve*, 1943

and Devolve (fig. 16) and *Forest Forms* (fig. 17) combine various aspects of Surrealism, most notably automatism and biomorphism as exemplified by André Masson, Joan Miró, and Matta, as well as the overlapping transparent veils of color seen in the work of Matta. Like many of the Abstract Expressionists, Kamrowski was interested in natural science and scientific drawings and models, and he was inspired by displays at the American Museum of Natural History in New York and also by books such as D'Arcy Thompson's *On Growth and Form* of 1917.[1] These sources inspired the nature-derived imagery and titles of his technically complex and densely detailed compositions.

The title *Revolve and Devolve* suggests an image in the process of transformation over time, and it alludes to the present's relationship with the primordial past, an idea held in common by many of the Abstract Expressionists during the 1940s, notably Barnett Newman, Adolph Gottlieb, and Mark Rothko. Within this primeval landscape, a horse and rider seem to emerge from the darkness and refresh themselves at a rippling stream of water, a symbolic giver of life. The sense of mystery is enhanced by the dramatic use of dark and light, accompanied by evocative halftones. The tonal range in *Revolve and Devolve* is extraordinary and is achieved solely from mixtures of black and white. Areas of deep black and sharp white are modulated with a wide variety of grays and tans. The smoky tonalities, along with the biomorphic shapes that emerge from within them, evoke the mood of a dreamscape, and the neutral and subdued colors suggest timeworn earth and rock. In 1983, Kamrowski spoke about his work of the 1940s: "I think it's a psychological integration, reflecting a simultaneity in nature—a process that binds all things together. A kind of cosmic rhythm rather than just a naturalistic object-figure-ground relationship. My early Surrealist works [refer to] . . . a whole chain of descendancy or ascendancy that occurs in a dialectical relationship."[2]

Experimentation with a variety of techniques and media was central for Kamrowski during the early 1940s, when he did much of his work on paper. Several different avenues of exploration are often reflected in a single picture. In *Revolve and Devolve*, he placed cutout shapes of paper over a wash of pale gray that he mottled with darker stains of gray and black. Most of these shapes, which are primarily rectangular or oval, are visible along the upper and lower borders of the composition. Next, Kamrowski brushed and rubbed another, more opaque layer of gray-black paint across the page.

17. *Forest Forms*, 1943

When the cutouts were removed, the areas that were covered retained the original ground-color. These "holes" in the painted layer, which relate to Kamrowski's collage shadow boxes of 1940 to 1943, create the illusion of deep space. They are distinguished from the shapes drawn by hand by their sharp straight edges. In other areas of the picture, the artist either allowed the paint to flow more freely or applied it with a brush. Painted or drawn lines are used both to create new shapes and to define the forms that are only suggested in the randomly patterned areas, and dotted lines suggest the passage of time and the movement of forms in space.

In Kamrowski's art, and also in the work of his Abstract Expressionist contemporaries, overlapping layers are used to suggest the possibility of a variety of interpretations. Among the multiple sources of this idea is James Joyce, whose writings were much admired by these artists. Kamrowski said of Joyce that his "idea of a multilayered and metaphysical image in the medium of the English language was probably the strongest thing of its time."[3] In *Forest Forms*, there are many layers, from the outer ones of blue, black, and purple opaque gouache to the innermost spaces seen through the "holes," which contain complex patterns on a transparent rose-colored ground. Most prominent among these patterns are the diffuse black lines that look like hairy worms, amoebas, or some sort of underwater flora. These may have been made by dropping diluted paint on paper and then blowing on it through a straw to move the medium around, a method used by Kamrowski's friend Jimmy Ernst, or they could be the result of applying paint to a surface already painted with an incompatible medium, a process that would cause the newly applied paint to spread out.

Throughout *Forest Forms*, there are many contrasts —between soft and sharp edges, between patterned and plain surfaces, and between recessive space and geometric flatness. It is as if one is trapped in limbo by the artist's contradictory illusions of form and space; one feels unable to escape the swirling vortex of leaflike shapes that lead to a centrally located spiderweb. In both style and imagery, this work is closely allied with the Surrealist pictures made by André Masson while he was in the United States from 1941 to 1945. Although Masson primarily stayed with the Surrealist enclave in Connecticut, his work was seen in exhibitions and publications in New York and had a great effect on the American avant-garde. Kamrowski acknowledged: "I obviously think American painters in the '40s were influenced by Masson. For the kind of things American painters were concerned with—and morphogenetics were one aspect of it—Masson was certainly the freest painter."[4]

In 1943, Kamrowski was experimenting with many different ideas and techniques. He noted of this period that "no one was concerned with turning out an identity commodity. You were subject to many influences and pursued many different things, you didn't work in a consistent line. It was a matter of trying to get some self-actualization and looking for an integration."[5] Kamrowski's Surrealist-inspired activities were the main incentive for his experiments; he spoke of automatist techniques as "a springboard for the imagination."[6] In accounts of painting in New York in the early 1940s, Kamrowski is noted as one of the first three painters—the other two are Baziotes and Pollock—to collaborate on a painting using a drip technique in about 1940–41.[7] He is also among the first to make large-scale paintings, and the works on paper demonstrate a tendency toward more monumental imagery and scale.

The year 1943 was one of great innovation and productivity for Kamrowski, and it also marked the beginning of his recognition by galleries and writers. Peggy Guggenheim included his work in the international collage show at her Art of This Century gallery, along with Baziotes, Robert Motherwell, Pollock, and Ad Reinhardt, and he also showed with Baziotes and Pollock in the exhibition "Abstract and Surrealist Painting" at the Sidney Janis Gallery. Two of his drawings were illustrated in the March issue of the art magazine *VVV*, and he was married for the first time early in the year. It was a promising time for a young artist who was not yet thirty. He continued to work in a Surrealist-inspired style throughout his stay in New York City until 1946 and afterward, well into the 1950s, after he had settled into a teaching job in Michigan. During the early 1940s, Kamrowski could be counted among the avant-garde, and in 1947, he was still grouped with the Abstract Expressionists in an exhibition and catalogue titled *Abstract Painting and Sculpture in America*, in the chapter called "Expressionist Biomorphic" with Baziotes, James Brooks, Arshile Gorky, Willem de Kooning, Pollock, Richard Pousette-Dart, Rothko, and Theodoros Stamos. But in the long term, he was eliminated from most accounts of early Abstract Expressionism because of his protracted affiliation with Surrealism after the 1940s. Yet, as these gouaches testify, Kamrowski is one of the most undervalued artists of that period.

1. Many of the Abstract Expressionists regularly visited the American Museum of Natural History, including Baziotes, Gottlieb, Newman, Rothko, and Stamos. Many artists also read and discussed D'Arcy Thompson's book during the 1940s, notably Tony Smith, who was a friend of Kamrowski's.

2. Gerome Kamrowski, quoted from "Gerome Kamrowski: An Interview with the Artist," Evan M. Maurer and Jennifer L. Bayles, *Gerome Kamrowski: A Retrospective Exhibition,* exh. cat., The University of Michigan Museum of Art (Ann Arbor, Michigan, 1983), p. 2.

3. Ibid., p. 3.

4. Ibid., p. 2.

5. Kamrowski, quoted from Martica Sawin, "Gerome Kamrowski: 'The Most Surrealist of Us All,'" *Arts Magazine* 62 (December 1987), p. 76.

6. Maurer and Bayles, p. 2.

7. See Jeffrey Wechsler, "Surrealism's Automatic Painting Lesson," *Art News* 76 (April 1977), pp. 45–46; Martica Sawin, "'The Third Man,' or Automatism American Style," *Art Journal* (Fall 1988), p. 181; and John Barron, "The Lion in Winter," *Detroit Monthly* (February 1990), pp. 56–57. See also the essay in this volume on William Baziotes.

Franz Kline
1910–1962

18. Untitled, ca. 1950

Brush and ink on paper

18 × 21 in. (45.7 × 53.3 cm)

Anonymous Loan

19. *Painted Newsprint,* 1948–50

Oil on newspaper, mounted on gessoed
cardboard

30 × 40 in. (76.2 × 101.6 cm)

Gift of Mr. and Mrs. William B. Jaffe, 1964 (64.305)

20. Untitled, ca. 1956

Oil, brush and ink, and cut, torn, and
pasted paper on paper

10¼ × 10¼ in. (26 × 26 cm)

Gift of Renée and David McKee, 1984 (1984.554.1)

21. *Black Reflections,* 1959

Oil and pasted paper on paper, mounted
on Masonite

19 × 19⅜ in. (48.3 × 49.2 cm)

Gift of Mr. and Mrs. Norman Schneider, 1964
(1964.146)

22. Study for *Flanders,* 1961

Brush and ink, and oil on paper

9 × 7⅛ in. (22.9 × 18.1 cm)

Gift of Renée and David McKee, 1984 (1984.554.2)

Franz Kline's ascension to a major place in first-generation
Abstract Expressionism in 1950–51 was something of a sur-
prise. Whereas the other major artists in the movement had
been through a decade of experimentation and refinement
and had reached their mature phase during the late 1940s,
Kline was making American-scene-type paintings of local

landscapes and portraits throughout the 1940s. Surrealism had never played a part in his development, nor did the work of Picasso, except in an oblique way, via Kline's interactions with other artists in New York City, where he had settled in 1938. Among the artists Kline knew early on are the painters Willem de Kooning, Philip Guston, Conrad Marca-Relli, and Bradley Walker Tomlin, and the photographer Aaron Siskind.

In May 1950, Clement Greenberg and Meyer Schapiro included Kline in their "Talent 1950" exhibition at the Samuel Kootz Gallery. Thomas B. Hess and Weldon Kees wrote favorably about Kline's work, but their reviews amounted to little more than a listing of the show's best artists.[1] In October 1950, Kline showed his large black-and-white abstractions in his first one-person exhibition at the Charles Egan Gallery. Kline was catapulted to what Frank O'Hara was to call "a stellar position . . . he took a firm, if controversial place in the consciousness of artists and collectors. Public recognition was slower to come, but his next exhibition a year later placed Kline in the company of Pollock, de Kooning, Gottlieb, Rothko, and Still, as one of the formative elements in a cultural development."[2] Kline's new work epitomized many salient aspects of Abstract Expressionism: large scale, aggressively gestural brushwork, sweeping allover multireferential imagery, and compressed space.

Kline and Willem de Kooning became good friends in 1943, and the two artists remained close until Kline's death in 1962. At de Kooning's studio, in 1948 or 1949, Kline first saw some of his small drawings enlarged with the aid of a Bell-Opticon machine. It was this event that confirmed Kline's explorations toward large-scale abstraction. This move is exemplified in Kline's untitled of ca. 1950 (fig. 18), in which black ink is brushed on white paper to create an open linear configuration. The circular shape in this composition is unusual in Kline's oeuvre but recurs in several of his paintings of the same period, such as *Chief* and *Clockface*.[3] His use of black and white also relates to works of the 1940s by de Kooning and Jackson Pollock.

As a result of his October 1950 exhibition, Kline became known as "the black-and-white artist." The label often caused confusion. As Kline stated, in an effort to discredit the notion that his work is related to Oriental calligraphy, "People sometimes think I take a white canvas and paint a black sign on it, but this is not true. I paint the white as well as the black, and the white is just as important."[4] Kline's point is clearly seen in *Painted Newsprint* of 1948–50 (fig. 19),[5] in which

18. Untitled, ca. 1950

the painted white areas clearly and uncharacteristically have dominance over the muted black lines. As he did in many of his pictures, Kline used several different tones of white paint here to achieve subtle nuances of surface texture, frequently mixing commercial paints with artist's paints. The work was made on a double spread of a newspaper's "help wanted" ads,[6] and it should be noted that when Kline made this work, the color of the newsprint, which has since darkened to a deep orange-brown, provided an additional shade of white.

It was not uncommon for one of Kline's own pictures to help spark the idea for another. Many times, Kline turned to his earlier paintings and studies, thus creating an unusual continuity in his work. Elaine de Kooning noted in 1962 that his paintings "seem like different versions of one immense, complicated machine seen from different angles."[7] A comparison of *Painted Newsprint* with Kline's American-scene painting *Old Sephardic Cemetery in Chinatown* of 1948[8] suggests a relationship between the central image of billowing sheets hanging over the graveyard in the earlier work and the abstract imagery in the later one. With only a few sweeps and spatters of black oil paint and rapid brushings of thick and diluted white around and over the black, Kline achieved the essential feeling of the movement and architectural structure that exists specifically in his representational picture.

The composition of Kline's untitled of ca. 1956 (fig. 20) suggests the possibility that the marinescapes of Albert Pinkham Ryder were among the many associations in Kline's memory when he made this painted collage. Like most of the other Abstract Expressionist artists, Kline was a regular visitor to The Metropolitan Museum of Art, about which he said: "You don't have to go see it all the time, but it's great to know it's around."[9] In addition to the Old Masters and the European modernists, Kline studied the work of Ryder, and he could have seen the nineteenth-century American romantic painter's *The Toilers of the Sea* at the Metropolitan Museum or in the Museum's March 1954 *Bulletin*.[10] In both similarly sized works, a square is divided into two roughly equal horizontal areas, and the Kline is evocative of Ryder's sky and sea imagery. Moving diagonally through the lower center of the Kline is a dark boomerang form surrounded by jagged white areas that is suggestive of the dark boat surrounded by moonlit waves similarly positioned in the Ryder.

Kline often used the imagery from his small works on paper as bases for his large painted canvases. In some instances, he actually attempted to copy the gestural lines stroke

19. *Painted Newsprint,* 1948–50

20. Untitled, ca. 1956

21. *Black Reflections*, 1959

for stroke in expanded scale, and although those canvases lack some of the spontaneity of the papers, they deliver considerable impact by virtue of their enormous size. Study for *Flanders* of 1961 (fig. 22) is one of Kline's works on paper that he translated into a large-scale version on canvas. This diminutive but powerful work is filled with discoveries that occur accidentally through the process of painting; marks are drawn quickly and then altered just as quickly. The black T-shape that appears in both the paper and the canvas has been interpreted by some as a human figure, and, more specifically, as a crucifix. Kline acknowledged the existence of figurative references in his abstract forms: "There are forms that are figurative to me, and if they develop into a figurative image . . . it's all right if they do. I don't have the feeling that something has to be completely non-associative as far as figure form is concerned."[11] The content underlying Kline's black-and-white abstractions is open to viewer interpretation. His pictures have also been related to the urban environment in which he lived.[12] Kline himself spoke about the emotive content conveyed by city sights: "When I look out the window —I've always lived in the city—I don't see trees in bloom or mountain laurel. What I do see—or rather, not what I see but the feelings aroused in me by that looking—is what I paint."[13]

Black Reflections of 1959 (fig. 21) is a small colorful oil on paper that bears an interesting relationship to a black-and-white untitled painting of 1954.[14] The 1954 painting has been hung both vertically and horizontally, and when viewed horizontally, the black triangle in the painting is a mirror image of the central shape in *Black Reflections*. The small oil is brightly colored with yellow, red, and green, in addition to black. The sudden reintroduction of color in Kline's work in 1956 coincided with his move to a new gallery, Sidney Janis, and evolved from his need to convey expressive levels that cannot be achieved with black and white alone. Unfortunately, he would never have the chance to reach his full potential in this regard. Kline died from a heart condition in 1962; he was only fifty-one years old.

Kline was a prolific and masterful draftsman. At the time of his death, there were 475 works on paper still in his possession. That drawing played a central role in Kline's art is clear from his own words: "Painting is a form of drawing, and the painting I like has a form of drawing to it. I don't see how it could be disassociated from the nature of drawing."[15]

22. Study for *Flanders*, 1961

1. There were twenty-three artists in the show, including Elaine de Kooning.

2. Frank O'Hara, "Franz Kline Talking," *Evergreen Review Reader 1957–1967,* 1968; reprinted in Frank O'Hara, *Art Chronicles 1954–1966* (New York: George Braziller, 1975), p. 40.

3. *Chief,* 1950, oil on canvas, 58⅜ × 73½ in., Collection The Museum of Modern Art, New York; *Clockface,* 1950, oil on canvas, 36 × 30 in., Collection Mr. and Mrs. Robert Rowan. For references to other paintings that contain circles or ovals, see Harry F. Gaugh, *The Vital Gesture: Franz Kline* (New York: Abbeville Press, 1985), pp. 93, 96.

4. Franz Kline, quoted from Katharine Kuh, *The Artist's Voice: Talks with Seventeen Artists* (New York: Harper & Row, 1962), p. 144.

5. There are two signatures and two dates, 1948 and 1950, on this work, indicating that Kline first worked on the picture in 1948 and then again in 1950. It was perhaps in 1950 that Kline mounted the newspaper on a stiff cardboard backing, something he often did as a prelude to using an image on paper as the basis for a large canvas. In this case, however, no related canvas has been identified.

6. Between 1948 and 1950, Kline painted hundreds of studies on newspaper and on pages from telephone books.

7. Elaine de Kooning, "Franz Kline," *Franz Kline Memorial Exhibition,* exh. cat., Washington Gallery of Modern Art (Washington, D. C., 1962), p. 17.

8. *Old Sephardic Cemetery in Chinatown,* 1948, oil on canvas, 20 × 24 in., Collection Mr. and Mrs. I. David Orr.

9. Kline, quoted from Thomas B. Hess, "Editorial: Franz Kline, 1910–1962," *Art News* 61 (Summer 1962), p. 53.

10. Kline spoke about Ryder's work in a 1958 interview published in O'Hara, p. 49. Ryder's *The Toilers of the Sea,* early 1880s, oil on wood, 11½ × 12 in., has been in the collection of The Metropolitan Museum of Art since 1915. For a complete list of exhibitions and publications on the work, see Doreen Bolger Burke, *American Paintings in The Metropolitan Museum of Art* (New York: The Metropolitan Museum of Art, 1980), vol. III, pp. 16–17.

11. Kline, quoted from David Sylvester, "Franz Kline 1910–1962: An Interview with David Sylvester," *Living Arts* 1 (1963), p. 10.

12. See, for example, John Gordon, *Franz Kline 1910–1962,* exh. cat., Whitney Museum of American Art (New York, 1968), p. 9.

13. Kline, quoted from Selden Rodman, *Conversations with Artists* (New York: Devin-Adair Co., 1957), pp. 109–10.

14. Untitled, 1954, oil and house paint on canvas, 83⅛ × 66¼ in., Collection Donald B. Marron.

15. Kline, quoted from Sylvester, p. 10.

Robert Motherwell
1915–1991

23. *Lyric Suite Number 1,* 1965

Brush and ink on paper

11 × 9 in. (27.9 × 22.9 cm)

Anonymous Gift, 1966 (66.233.1)

24. *Lyric Suite Number 2,* 1965

Brush and ink on paper

11 × 9 in. (27.9 × 22.9 cm)

Anonymous Gift, 1966 (66.233.2)

25. *Lyric Suite Number 4,* 1965

Brush and ink on paper

11 × 9 in. (27.9 × 22.9 cm)

Anonymous Gift, 1966 (66.233.4)

26. *Lyric Suite Number 5,* 1965

Brush and ink on paper

11 × 9 in. (27.9 × 22.9 cm)

Anonymous Gift, 1966 (66.233.5)

Prior to 1941, Robert Motherwell studied philosophy, literature, and art history in various undergraduate and graduate programs in the United States and in France. Through the art historian Meyer Schapiro, with whom he studied art history at Columbia University in New York City in 1940, Motherwell became acquainted with the French Surrealists who had left Europe because of the war and were living in New York and Connecticut. He decided to leave academia and begin painting full time in 1941. Motherwell had little formal art training and never painted representational pictures. His earliest works are highly abstracted geometric and linear configurations of figures and interiors. By the late 1940s, his brushwork became considerably looser and more gestural, and his shapes more simplified and biomorphic.

Motherwell's affinity with French culture gave him easy entrée into the Surrealist circle. During the spring of 1941, he met the Chilean Surrealist Matta, and they traveled together that summer for three months in Mexico, where, Motherwell recalled in a 1967 interview, "Matta gave me a ten-year education in Surrealism. Through him I met Wolfgang Paalen, a prominent Surrealist, who was living in Mexico City...and it was with him that I got my postgraduate education in Surrealism, so to speak."[1] When he returned to New York, Motherwell began to meet the American artists who were also interested in Surrealist ideas and techniques. Matta introduced him to William Baziotes, with whom he quickly developed a rapport that was of great import for both artists and for the development of Abstract Expressionist ideas and art during the 1940s.[2] By the mid-1940s, Motherwell's acquaintances included Willem de Kooning, Adolph Gottlieb, Jackson Pollock, and Mark Rothko. In Jackson Pollock's studio, in 1943, Motherwell made his first collages, marking the beginning of an extensive body of work that has earned him a position among the century's master collagists. Motherwell was a prolific artist, and over the next fifty years, he produced a vast number of paintings and works on paper, in addition to his many collages. He was also an eloquent writer and speaker, and, as such, he contributed greatly to the dissemination of Abstract Expressionist ideas and to the recording of its history firsthand.

Throughout his career, drawing was an essential component of Motherwell's art. He used it both to evolve new images for his paintings and to explore forms and pictorial issues that had emerged in his paintings. After 1945, Motherwell's works on paper were created almost exclusively with ink or paint applied with a brush. In 1948, he made a small black-and-white sketch composed of ovoids and rectangles that marked the starting point for his large and important series of paintings and drawings called *Elegies to the Spanish Republic*, abstract statements of universal content that generated a major source of inspiration for Motherwell's mature Abstract Expressionist oeuvre. In a 1946 statement titled "Beyond the Aesthetic," Motherwell expressed the idea that is central to all his work: "To find or invent 'objects' (which are more strictly speaking relational structures) whose felt quality satisfies the passions—that for me is the activity of the artist, an activity which does not cease even in sleep. No wonder the artist is constantly placing and displacing, relating and rupturing relations; his task is to find a complex of

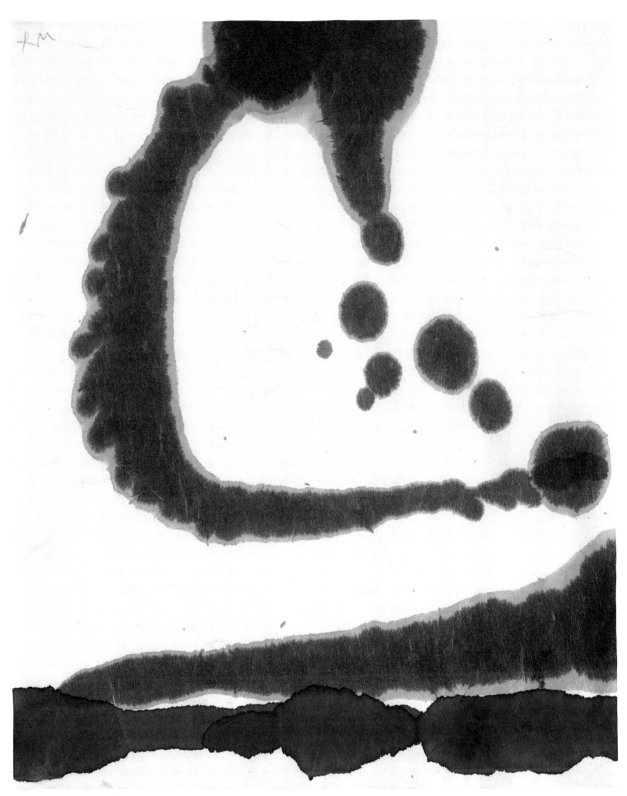

23. *Lyric Suite Number 1*, 1965

qualities whose feeling is just right—veering toward the unknown and chaos, yet ordered and related in order to be apprehended."[3]

The death of Motherwell's close friend David Smith on May 23, 1965, in an automobile accident brought a sudden and final end to a cycle of drawings Motherwell had begun early that April. He had intended to produce one thousand pieces, but he had completed only 565. The series is titled *Lyric Suite* (see figs. 23 to 26), after the string quartet by Alban Berg that Motherwell listened to repeatedly while working on these pictures. The general format of these works is similar to that of Motherwell's 1962 series titled *Beside the Sea,* which was done with oil paint on large sheets of laminated rag paper. In both cycles, a strong horizontal line, or lines, usually at the bottom of the page, counterbalances the large irregular blobs and spatterings that activate the major portion of the sheet.

Motherwell found inspiration in the ideas and methods of Zen painting, which, while discussing the *Lyric Suite* series, he described as "unadulterated automatism. I took a thousand identical sheets of Japanese rice paper, an English watercolor brush, and common American inks, and worked perhaps forty at a session, without conscious preconceptions, and with no revision—that was the rule of the game."[4] The nine-by-eleven-inch sheets were placed around the floor; some were done with quick darting motions, and others with slow and flowing ones. Chance effects happened as the ink spread quickly through the loose fibers of the rice paper and swelled greatly; the components of the black ink separated into grayish-blue areas with orange, red, or violet halos around them, while the blue ink remained vibrant. In much of his work, Motherwell relied heavily on black and white, which he called the "protagonists" in his pictures, even when color was introduced. His works on paper in particular are generally stark displays of gestural black marks on white paper. In the *Lyric Suite* works, however, the textured absorbency of the lightweight rice paper caused the edges to blur and create a very different effect. This uncharacteristic use of an absorbent support is perhaps related to the contemporaneous paintings on unsized canvas of Helen Frankenthaler, Morris Louis, and Kenneth Noland.

Motherwell remarked about the process he followed in the *Lyric Suite* series: "Paint the thousand sheets without

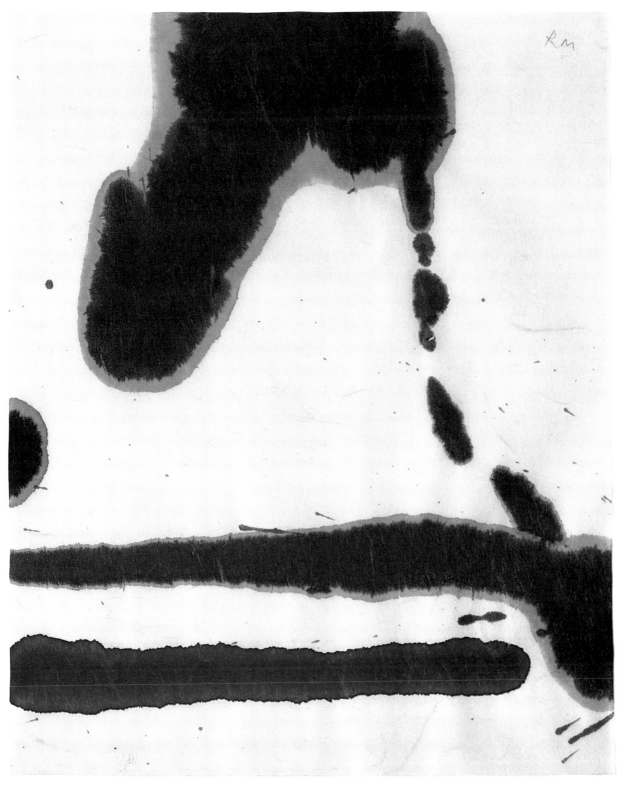

24. *Lyric Suite Number 2*, 1965

interruption, without a priori traditional or moral prejudices or a posteriori ones, without iconography, and above all without revisions or additions upon critical reflection and judgment and see what lies within, whatever it is. Venture. Don't look back. Do not tire. Everything is open. Brushes and blank white paper."[5] The motion is direct; the image is unmodified; the singular gesture links the artist and the image metaphysically, as it does for the Zen painter. As in all Abstract Expressionist works of art, it is central that the artist be so skilled that the image happens automatically but also with the control that comes from knowledge of the painterly process. And also as in all Abstract Expressionist art, the image is an abstract visualization of an emotion; in one form, it links the most personal and the universal. Motherwell said in 1982 that the artist's hand takes off "by itself, so to speak . . . it is close to . . . mindlessness, or to pure essences with nothing between your beingness and the external world. . . . It is more what you unconsciously know than what you think."[6] Many of the Abstract Expressionists had an affinity with Zen painting and ideas—Franz Kline, David Smith, and Theodoros Stamos, for example—and it was one of many mutually held influences among these artists who maintained a continual dialogue throughout the 1940s and into the 1950s. This artistic interchange is reflected in the connection between Motherwell's art and that of David Smith, a relationship that has never been fully explored but is indicated by the works on paper in this selection.

Motherwell's spontaneous gestures convey the great exhilaration and sense of freedom he got from drawing, which was for him "perhaps the only medium as fast as the mind itself."[7] In the *Lyric Suite* series, he gave his unconscious free rein. Through them, we become the intimate witnesses of an extraordinary range of invention produced with the simplest of means.

1. Robert Motherwell, quoted from Sidney Simon, "Concerning the Beginnings of the New York School: 1939–1943—An Interview Conducted with Robert Motherwell by Sydney Simon," *Art International* II (Summer 1967), p. 21.

2. For more information, see the essay in this volume on William Baziotes.

3. Motherwell, quoted from "Beyond the Aesthetic," *Design* 47, no. 8 (April 1946), p. 14.

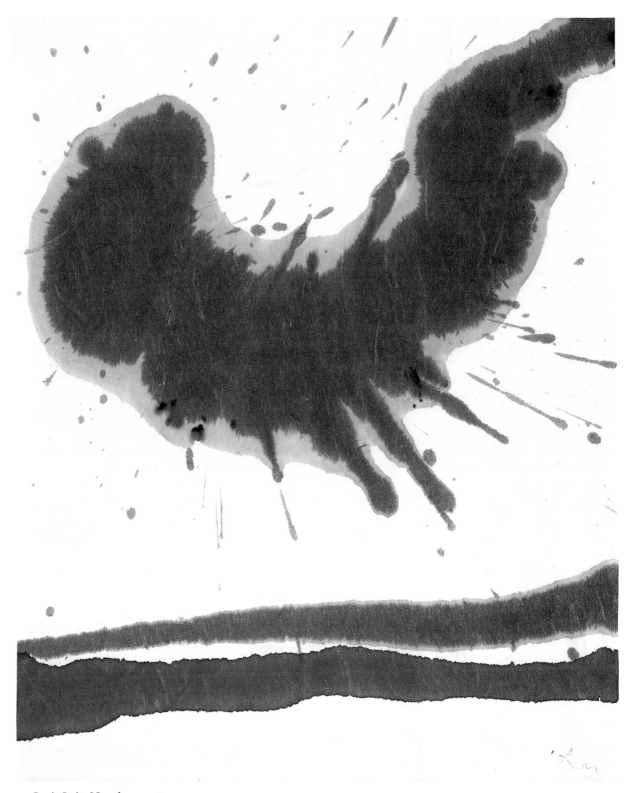

25. *Lyric Suite Number 4*, 1965

4. Motherwell, quoted from H. H. Arnason, *Robert Motherwell*, 2nd ed. (New York: Harry N. Abrams, Inc., 1982), p. 154.

5. Motherwell, quoted from Robert C. Hobbs, "Robert Motherwell's Open Series," *Robert Motherwell,* exh. cat., Städtische Kunsthalle (Dusseldorf, 1976), p. 48.

6. Motherwell, quoted from Jack D. Flam, "With Robert Motherwell," Dore Ashton and Jack D. Flam, *Robert Motherwell,* Albright-Knox Art Gallery, exh. cat. (New York: Abbeville Press, 1983), pp. 23, 25.

7. Motherwell in 1970, quoted from "Thoughts on Drawing," *The Drawing Society National Exhibition 1970*, exh. cat., The American Federation of Arts (New York, 1970), n.p.

26. *Lyric Suite Number 5*, 1965

Barnett Newman
1905–1970

27. *The Song of Orpheus,* 1944–45
Oil pastel on paper
20 × 14⅞ in. (50.8 × 37.8 cm)
Gift of Annalee Newman, 1992 (1992.179.1)

28. Untitled, 1945
Brush and ink on paper
19⅞ × 14¾ in. (50.5 × 37.5 cm)
Gift of Annalee Newman, 1992 (1992.179.3)

29. Untitled, 1945
Oil pastel on paper
11½ × 16¼ in. (29.2 × 41.3 cm)
Gift of Annalee Newman, 1992 (1992.179.2)

30. Untitled, 1960
Brush and ink on paper
14 × 10 in. (35.6 × 25.4 cm)
Gift of Annalee Newman, 1992 (1992.179.4)

It was as a writer and a philosopher that Barnett Newman first came to prominence from the late 1930s to the mid-1940s within the Abstract Expressionist circle that included Adolph Gottlieb and Mark Rothko. His impassioned articles, letters, catalogue introductions, and position statements explained the reasoning behind their belief that modern abstract art should convey the same power as primitive art and myth. His probing analyses of Precolumbian sculpture, Oceanic art, Northwest Coast Indian painting, Neo-Plasticism, and Surrealism identified some of the sources assimilated by the Abstract Expressionists. In his early writings, Newman was generous in his praise of such painters as Gottlieb, Rothko, and Theodoros Stamos. Yet, although Newman produced many notable images during the 1940s, including an extensive body of works on paper, his own recognition as an artist did not occur until much later, in the late 1950s to early

27. *The Song of Orpheus*, 1944–45

1960s, when his "zip" paintings were hailed as a precursor of color-field painting and minimalist art.

In 1945, after many years of study, working in the family clothing business, and substitute teaching, Newman focused his creative energies completely on painting, although he continued to write as well. During the early 1940s, he had made a number of drawings, which he later destroyed. Between 1946 and 1950, his work was shown in six group exhibitions, including the historic 1947 "Ideographic Picture" that he organized at the Betty Parsons Gallery. By 1948, he had developed his mature format, in which a minimum of pictorial means achieves innovative and moving results. These works consist of large fields of single color articulated by vertical bands, or "zips," as he called them. Their apparent simplicity made their meaning difficult to understand. Even Newman's fellow artists found them hard to comprehend, and as a result of this, combined with the problems of competing egos and artistic territoriality, Newman did not find the support he expected within the Abstract Expressionist group. In 1950 and again in 1951, Newman had one-person exhibitions at the Parsons Gallery. They were deeply disappointing to him, as both artists and critics dismissed the work either through indifference or with outright contempt. As a result of such affronts, Newman's longstanding friendships with Gottlieb, Rothko, and Clyfford Still soon cooled. Only Jackson Pollock and Tony Smith expressed appreciation of Newman's vision and maintained an exchange of ideas with him during the ensuing years. It was not until seven years after his 1951 show that Newman was given another solo exhibition. It was for the next generation of artists and critics to recognize his singular contribution to Abstract Expressionism.

During the early to mid-1940s, Newman concentrated on drawing as a means of formulating imagery that would develop ideas he had already expressed in his writings, and he produced almost no paintings.[1] These early drawings were very private discoveries for Newman, and he did not show them to his artist friends at the time. He kept thirty sheets from 1944–45; they were made with a variety of media—oil, pastel, ink, and watercolor—and account for more than one-third of his total recorded output of drawings.[2]

Newman's 1945 untitled brush-and-ink drawing of an abstracted head (fig. 28) exemplifies a motif that appeared very briefly, and only in his drawings.[3] The face is masklike; each feature is indicated by an abstract schematized symbol. The nose, for example, is a blackened triangle, and the mouth is

28. Untitled, 1945

a long rectangular bar with short black dashes for teeth. One eye is a wide-open circle with a small pupil, while the other seems to be shut in a jagged wink. The chin is a wide V-shape that ends in two black circles. The entire image is fierce and rough, suggesting a source in the primitive art that Newman studied and wrote about during the 1940s. The black outlines and the segmented features have affinities with the art of the Northwest Coast Indians.[4] In addition to his interest in primitive art, Newman also may have been thinking of André Masson's fluid graphic handling of brush and ink in this Surrealist's personages of the early to mid-1940s.[5] The paintings and drawings Masson produced while he was living in the United States were exhibited several times in 1944–45 in New York museums and galleries, where they were very likely seen by Newman.

The Song of Orpheus of 1944–45 (fig. 27) is one of only four drawings from this period that Newman titled and one of only eight known drawings that he signed. Many podlike shapes quiver on the surface, like motile amoebas under a microscope. The generally brown and yellow coloring suggests the earth, and the wriggling black, brown, and green circle and vertical lines evoke seedlings and roots growing underground. The work is drawn with oil pastels that have been applied in a variety of ways—heavily pressed on the paper, lightly rubbed and/or smeared, and dragged on their sides over the paper in a circular motion that creates fanlike wedges. The texture of the paper itself further adds to the picture's tactility. As in many of Newman's works of this period, there is no specified horizon line and no specifically identifiable imagery. The forms float freely in space with no definite spatial orientation, and it is quite possible that Newman worked on this sheet from several different directions. Only the placement of his signature indicates a prescribed point of view.

The title *The Song of Orpheus* refers to the mythic Greek poet who was famed for his skill with a lyre. With the divine power of his music, he was able to bring back his wife, Eurydice, from the dead, but through his human failings, he lost her again and ultimately caused his own horrible death. It has alternately been proposed that Newman chose the Orpheus legend because of his concern with tragedy or as an autobiographical reference to his personal regeneration after dedicating himself to painting,[6] but the fanciful nature of this picture's organic and inorganic components suggests another interpretation. According to the myth, Orpheus's musical powers were so extraordinary that he "charmed not

29. Untitled, 1945

only the wild beasts but also the trees and the rocks which would come after him at the sound of his lyre."[7] It is just such a divine union of man, animal, earth, and plant that Newman's drawing conveys.

Both *The Song of Orpheus* and the untitled oil pastel of 1945 (fig. 29) recall Newman's interest in the natural sciences. Between 1939 and 1941, he took courses at the Brooklyn Botanical Garden, vacationed at the Audubon Nature Camp in Maine, and attended summer classes in botany and ornithology at Cornell University. The imagery in these two drawings obviously relates to visual sources that Newman experienced from such activities. The untitled oil pastel is composed of blocks of color in which only a few clinging tendrils and leaves grow in odd directions. Both in its imagery and in the rough handling of the pastels, this work has a tentative quality that gives it a particular immediacy and intimacy. Once again, the orientation is ambiguous, but here, the structure of the composition is anchored by the dominant presence of the rectangular blocks. Although the shapes are relatively flat, they do convey a sense of mass and space.

The simplified composition of the 1945 oil pastel, and more specifically the blocks of color, seem to prefigure the appearance of Newman's first zip pictures, just a few years later, in 1948. It has been noted more than once that, as Paul Schimmel put it, "Newman ultimately discarded the biological details of the foreground in favor of the abstraction of the background."[8] While this theory is plausible, it de-emphasizes the complex change that took place in Newman's artistic concept. He did not paint geometric abstractions but rather created pictures in which space alone, without the aid of narrative details, conveyed meaning. In 1962, Newman explained: "Instead of using outlines, instead of making shapes or setting off spaces my drawing declares the space."[9] The zip, which appears variously as either a wide band or a thin line, was, as Newman said, "a field that brings life to the other fields, just as the other fields bring life to this so-called line."[10] At first, the colored field and the zip are perceived separately, and upon contemplation, they are seen simultaneously. Thomas Hess wrote in 1969: "You see the zip as a division, and the color it divides becomes the main actor in the painting; or, you see the zip as the point of focus and the large color areas as its medium; finally, you see both ways."[11] "Their simultaneous comprehension creates that third thing, which is the finished painting."[12]

Newman's untitled drawing of 1960 (fig. 30) is a single

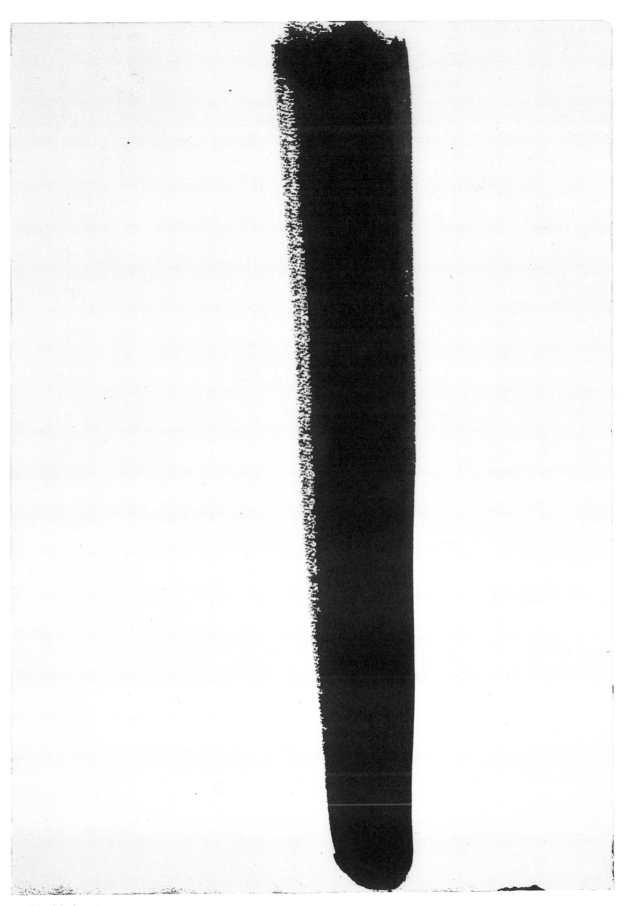

30. Untitled, 1960

black brushstroke of ink, the zip, in the middle of the unpainted white paper. Apparently, the stroke was made with a fairly wide brush whose bristles splayed out slightly as the gesture was completed, making one end wider than the other. The motion seems to have been started at the narrow, somewhat rounded tip, where the ink is densest. It is unclear whether Newman brought the stroke upward from the bottom as it is represented here, or made the gesture downward and then turned the paper to its present position. Similar tapered zips first appeared in Newman's drawings in 1945–46; in these, the colors are in reverse—the zip is unpainted white paper, and the surrounding field is painted black. It has been suggested by Hess that this format may have arisen in Newman's unconscious through his knowledge of a painting in the Metropolitan Museum's collection, Jonas Lie's *The Conquerors (Culebra Cut, Panama Canal)* of 1913, in which strong black lines of smoke waft upward.[13]

Untitled of 1960 is one of a group of twenty-two black-and-white drawings Newman made that year, all of which are black ink on watercolor paper that is either ten by fourteen inches or nine by twelve inches in size. They were produced during the period of his fourteen *Stations of the Cross* canvases, which date from between 1958 and 1966 and also used a palette of black and white. Subsequent to this 1960 group, Newman produced only one more drawing, in 1969, for an exhibition titled "The Big Drawing" at the Graham Gallery in New York.

In most of Newman's paintings and drawings, the zips continue to the two edges of the field and evoke a sense of continuity beyond these borders. Untitled of 1960 is highly unusual in this regard, and the zip's monolithic presence suggests a correlation with the small number of sculptures that Newman created late in his career, between 1962 and 1969. Of particular note in this regard is *Here III* of 1966, a single metal zip that incorporates and activates the space around it, and Newman's most famous sculpture, *Broken Obelisk* of 1963–67, in which the inverted obelisk's tip recalls the tapered shape of the black zip in Newman's 1960 drawing.

1. According to Thomas B. Hess, *Barnett Newman*, exh. cat., The Museum of Modern Art (New York, 1971), p. 45, Barnett Newman destroyed all the work he made prior to 1944.

2. According to Brenda Richardson, *Barnett Newman: The Complete Drawings, 1944–1969*, exh. cat., The Baltimore Museum of Art (Baltimore, Md., 1977), pp. 17–18, Newman preserved a total of eighty-three drawings made between 1944 and 1969.

3. Only one other head is catalogued; see Richardson, cat. no. 21. Several other black-and-white ink drawings, also from 1945 and done on the same size paper, use similar pictorial symbols within the context of landscapes or organic abstractions; see Richardson, cat. nos. 23–28.

4. See head painted on drum illustrated in W. Jackson Rushing, "The Impact of Nietzsche and Northwest Coast Indian Art on Barnett Newman's Idea of Redemption in the Abstract Sublime," *Art Journal* 47, no. 3 (Fall 1988), p. 191; and Chilkat blankets, one of which is illustrated in Stephen Polcari, *Abstract Expressionism and the Modern Experience* (Cambridge: Cambridge University Press, 1991), p. 193.

5. One of Masson's watercolor-and-ink drawings of 1944, *Regardent l'aquarium*, 19¾ × 23½ in., collection Anne and Jean-Claude Lahumiere, is particularly close to Newman's rendering of the facial features. See Masson illustrated in *The Interpretive Link: Abstract Surrealism into Abstract Expressionism, Works on Paper 1938–1948*, exh. cat., Newport Harbor Art Museum (Newport Harbor, Ca., 1986), p. 111.

6. See Rushing, p. 192, and Hess, pp. 45, 47.

7. James Hall, *Dictionary of Subjects and Symbols in Art* (New York: Harper & Row, 1979), p. 230.

8. Paul Schimmel, "Images of Metamorphosis," *The Interpretive Link*, p. 25.

9. Newman, quoted from an interview with Dorothy Gees Seckler titled "Frontiers of Space," *Art in America* 50, no. 2 (Summer 1962); reprinted in John P. O'Neill, ed., *Barnett Newman: Selected Writings and Interviews* (New York: Alfred A. Knopf, 1990), p. 251.

10. Newman, quoted from an interview with David Sylvester, broadcast on the BBC, November 17, 1965; published in *The Listener*, August 10, 1972; reprinted in O'Neill, p. 256.

11. Thomas B. Hess, *Barnett Newman* (New York: Walker and Co., 1969), p. 48.

12. Ibid.

13. Hess 1971, p. 49.

Jackson Pollock
1912–1956

31. Page from a sketchbook, ca. 1938
Brush and ink on paper
17⅝ × 13⅞ in. (44.8 × 35.2 cm)
Gift of Lee Krasner Pollock, 1982 (1982.147.14a,b)

32. Untitled, ca. 1945
Pen and ink, brush and ink, and colored
and watercolor pencils on paper board
15 × 11¼ in. (38.1 × 28.6 cm)
Gift of Lee Krasner Pollock, 1982 (1982.147.34)

33. *War*, 1947
Pen and ink, and colored pencils on paper
20⅝ × 26 in. (52.4 × 66 cm)
Gift of Lee Krasner Pollock, in memory of Jackson
Pollock, 1982 (1982.147.25)

34. Untitled, ca. 1947
Gouache, watercolor, colored watercolor
pencils, and pen and ink on paper
14 × 18⅝ in. (35.6 × 47.3 cm)
Gift of Lee Krasner Pollock, 1982 (1982.147.35)

35. Untitled, ca. 1948–49
Pen and ink, brush and ink, and graphite
pencil on paper
11 × 8⅜ in. (27.9 × 21.3 cm)
Gift of Lee Krasner Pollock, 1982 (1982.147.26)

36. Untitled, ca. 1950
Dripped ink on paper
18⅞ × 24¾ in. (47.9 × 62.9 cm)
Gift of Lee Krasner Pollock, 1982 (1982.147.28)

31. Page from a sketchbook, ca. 1938

37. Untitled, ca. 1952–56

Dripped ink on paper

28⅞ × 20⅞ in. (73.3 × 53 cm)

Gift of Lee Krasner Pollock, 1982 (1982.147.29)

38. Untitled, ca. 1952–56

Dripped ink on Howell paper

18⅛ × 21⅞ in. (46 × 55.6 cm)

Gift of Lee Krasner Pollock, 1982 (1982.147.30)

Jackson Pollock is the best-known Abstract Expressionist. From 1942, when he had his first one-person exhibition at Peggy Guggenheim's Art of This Century gallery in New York City, until his death in an automobile crash at age forty-four in 1956, Pollock's volatile art and personality made him a dominant figure in the art world and in the press. In 1947–48, Pollock achieved a radically new innovation; using drip and pour techniques that rely on a linear structure in both his canvases and papers, he created works that redefined the categories of drawing and painting. Referring to his 1951 exhibition at the Betty Parsons Gallery, fellow Abstract Expressionist painter Lee Krasner, who was also Pollock's wife, noted that his work "seemed like monumental drawing, or maybe painting with the immediacy of drawing—some new category."[1]

From the beginning of Pollock's career, drawing played a seminal role. Throughout his life, he kept many of his early sketchbooks and individual drawings in his studio, no matter how small the sheet or slight the image. The more than five hundred works on paper documented in the catalogue raisonné trace Pollock's dramatic evolution, which began in the early 1930s during his student days.[2] At that time, Pollock made many sketches from the model and landscapes on site, and he also used the medium to analyze Old Master compositions from reproductions in books. Such traditional methods were taught at the Art Students League in New York City, where Pollock studied from 1930 to 1933. His teacher there, Thomas Hart Benton, one of America's foremost Regionalist painters and muralists of the period, had a profound effect on Pollock's work. After he left the League, Pollock continued to use the exercise he had learned from Benton of analyzing the structure of Old Master paintings using geometric shape, line, and shadow. Numerous pencil sketches dating from the late 1930s to the early 1940s are

32. Untitled, ca. 1945

studies of figures from paintings by Rubens, Michelangelo, and El Greco. Pollock often drew several sketches after different paintings on the same sheet. Benton later remarked about Pollock: "In his analytical work he got things out of proportion, but found the essential rhythms."[3] During this period, while he was in Jungian analysis, Pollock also made many so-called analytical drawings in which he juxtaposed various individual images on one page.

During the early to mid-1930s, Pollock was also affected by the work of the Mexican mural painters José Clemente Orozco and David Alfaro Siqueiros. He was one of several young Americans who joined Siqueiros's workshop in New York in 1936. There he was exposed to unorthodox media and techniques such as enamel paints, spray guns, airbrushes, and poured paints. Although Pollock did not incorporate these elements into his work immediately, he was receptive to this kind of experimentation and drew on the experience in later work.

By the late 1930s, Pollock had developed a formal approach and a repertoire of imagery that could be considered a precursor to his mature work. In 1969, Lee Krasner said: "All of Jackson's work grows from the [sketches of the] thirties; I see no more sharp breaks, but rather a continuing development of the same themes and obsessions."[4] This selection of eight of the works on paper in the Museum's collection traces Pollock's artistic evolution from 1938 to 1956; they exemplify both the individuality of his route and his central place in Abstract Expressionism. They also suggest his extraordinary versatility in a variety of media. During the course of his career, Pollock used pencil, colored pencil, chalk, pastel, crayon, gouache, tempera, watercolor, watercolor pencil, ink, wax, enamel paint, and metallic paint. In addition to conventional drawing stock, he used cardboard, handmade rag paper, laminated wrapping paper, rice paper, sketchpad covers, and typing paper.

The Museum's page from a Pollock sketchbook of ca. 1938 (fig. 31) is composed of multiple primitivized animal and figure forms. The images are drawn with a brush in elegant flowing lines that thicken and thin, bend and turn, with great variety. In evidence is the strong influence of Picasso, and also of Paul Klee, Joan Miró, and American Indian art, in which narratives, when they occur, are sometimes depicted with schematized stick figures. These sources are already in a process of transformation in this analytical drawing, in which Pollock drew his archetypal imagery from his own subconscious. Unlike earlier works in which the various figures on

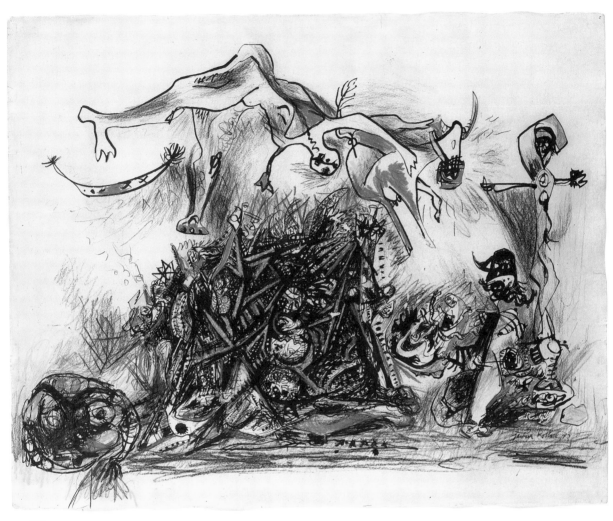

33. *War*, 1947

the page are unrelated, here they are elements in an allover composition and are united by an implied underlying irregular grid structure. Throughout the work, sexual connections between the various male-female, animal-human couples are evident. At the center, for example, the contours of a reclining female nude fit into those of the male horse beneath her like two connecting pieces of a jigsaw puzzle. As in many other drawings of the period, some of the figures —the kneeling woman at the upper left and the ghostly apparition beside her, for example—are oriented in different directions, suggesting that the artist worked on the sheet from various angles. It is a method more fully developed in Pollock's large drip paintings of the late 1940s and early 1950s, when he laid the canvas on the floor and physically moved into and around it as he worked.

It is interesting to compare Pollock's untitled drawing of ca. 1945 (fig. 32) with his large early masterpiece on canvas of 1943, *Pasiphaë*. Similar pairs of semiabstract totemic figures appear in both these works and also in other paintings and drawings of the period. Like the two sentinels in the painting, the two personages in the drawing emerge out of a dense mélange of curving lines and colored areas. The tinted areas in the drawing, made with watercolor pencils dipped into water and rubbed over the paper, have a painterly quality. Although it is evident in both media that the artist's gestural calligraphy spontaneously generates the forms, the drawing better displays the increasing role of chance and free association in Pollock's work.

Pollock's famous *War* (fig. 33) is the only drawing he ever titled, and it is inscribed "1947." In this complex composition, there are specific references to imagery found in Pollock's earlier works. For example, the linear drawings of a falling figure and bull at the top center here closely relate to the nude figure and bull in his drawing of ca. 1938 (see fig. 31),[5] and the dense thicket of shapes beneath these images on the present work resembles Pollock's drawings in sketchbooks of ca. 1939–40. The monstrous destruction of war is conveyed both by the fierceness of his graphic execution and by the imagery—hooded, falling, disembodied, and crucified figures, and the suggestion of a raging pyre. Some of the images are camouflaged by the many linear motions, which are darkened and thickened and highlighted with flashes of red and yellow pencil to further heighten the dramatic intensity. Even as this work communicates the universal horrors of war, it also evolves from Pollock's inner self. In 1947, Pollock said: "The unconscious is a very important side of

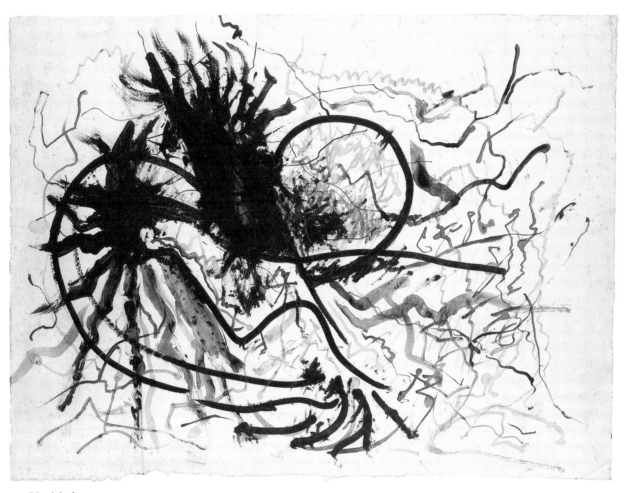

34. Untitled, ca. 1947

modern art and I think the unconscious drives do mean a lot in looking at paintings. My opinion is that new needs need new techniques. And the modern artists have found new ways and new means of making their statements. It seems to me that the modern painter cannot express this age, the airplane, the atom bomb, the radio, in the old forms of the Renaissance or of any other past culture. Each age finds its own technique."[6]

Two small untitled drawings, one of ca. 1947 (fig. 34) and the other of ca. 1948–49 (fig. 35), exemplify Pollock's move further into abstraction. Representational imagery is almost completely eliminated, and meaning is communicated through the forceful shapes and lines spontaneously generated by highly energetic calligraphic motions. In both works, improvised random markings cover the page, with certain shapes and lines emphasized in black. The process is similar to James Brooks's use of staining in 1948 and is related to Pollock's 1941 experiments with William Baziotes and Gerome Kamrowski, which are based on Surrealist concepts of automatism.

During the years from 1947 to 1950, Pollock produced 140 paintings, many of them mural-size, while he made fewer than fifty works on paper. His major preoccupation was with the large-scale dripped, poured, and spattered paintings done on unstretched canvas on the floor, which are considered by most his greatest achievements. Frank O'Hara wrote about these canvases in 1959: "There has never been enough said about Pollock's draftsmanship, that amazing ability to quicken a line by thinning it, to slow it by flooding, to elaborate that simplest of elements, the line—to change, to reinvigorate, to extend, to build up an embarrassment of riches in the mass of drawing alone."[7]

Pollock had already produced his first few drip and spatter paintings on canvas in 1946, but it was not until 1948 that he used this technique in his works on paper. His untitled paper of ca. 1950 (fig. 36) is one of a sequence of ten small black-ink drawings discovered in his studio after his death. In this fluid and open composition, spattered streaks of ink punctuated by dots and drips dance across the page. They are spontaneous and direct but also demonstrate the artist's control of every nuance of his gestures. While thicker paint was primarily poured in meandering skeins in the paintings of this period, the thinner ink used in the drawings encouraged spattering more than pouring. Referring to his black-and-white pictures of 1950 to 1953, Pollock used the term "drawing" to describe both his canvases and his works on paper.[8]

35. Untitled, ca. 1948–49

36. Untitled, ca. 1950

37. Untitled, ca. 1952–56

From 1952 until 1956, the last five years of his life, Pollock was extremely troubled both artistically and personally, and he produced relatively few works of art. Among his last are two untitled sheets, both of ca. 1952–56 (figs. 37 and 38) and both executed in black ink dripped onto the paper with the dropper of a bottle top. These drawings exhibit the reemergence that took place during that period of more recognizable imagery, including the large heads that also appear in his paintings after 1951. Frequently, the figurative references are obscured by elaborate calligraphy, as they are in the second of these two works, but sometimes they are left more exposed, as in the first. During the period he was making these works, Pollock stated: "I'm very representational some of the time, and a little all of the time. But when you're working out of your unconscious, figures are bound to emerge. We're all of us influenced by Freud, I guess. I've been Jungian for a long time.... Painting is a state of being.... Painting is self-discovery. Every good artist paints what he is."[9]

In the large work on Japanese rice paper (see fig. 37), flowing black linear motions delineate what appears to be a face, head, and body on the lefthand side of the composition. The abstracted figure is difficult to read, but one can make out an eye, a triangular nose, pronounced nostrils, and a patterned shirt. In the lower portion of the work, four roughly rectangular areas are filled with mysterious image-writing, and the pattern under the head also resembles rapidly conjured calligraphy. The effect of the thin dripped ink lines that mingle with the fibers of the rice paper is very similar to that achieved by the lines Pollock dripped with enamel paint on unprimed canvas.

The second untitled work (see fig. 38) is one of about fifteen drawings that Pollock made during the 1950s on sheets of handmade paper crafted by Douglass Howell. These densely textured papers are woven from one-hundred percent pure rag fibers—pieces of tablecloths, towels, and other linens—without the addition of glue, sizing, or chemicals. Depending on the mix of materials used, the sheets are either solid or multicolored.[10] The piece Pollock selected for this drawing is medium gray with small flecks of chartreuse, green, and beige running through it. There is one large piece of beige fabric, drawn over by Pollock, that eluded the shredding process. The entire surface is animated with patches and drips of dark black ink that sink into and spread out on the absorbent surface. Pollock's choice of paper adds to the denseness of the surface, amplifying the hermetic quality of

38. Untitled, ca. 1952–56

this work. The imagery is barely apparent, almost completely disguised by the heavy overlay of black gestures. Only the suggestion of a head remains visible at the upper left.

In 1950, Pollock made a statement that expresses both his formidable contribution and the underlying idea that informs all Abstract Expressionist art: "I approach painting in the same sense as one approaches drawing; that is, it's direct. I don't work from drawings. I don't make sketches and drawings and color sketches into a final painting. Painting, I think today—the more immediate, the more direct—the greater the possibilities of making a direct—of making a statement."[11]

1. Lee Krasner, quoted in B. H. Friedman, *Jackson Pollock: Energy Made Visible* (New York: McGraw-Hill, 1972), p. 182.

2. Pollock's total oeuvre, of 1930 to 1956, numbers almost 1,100 works in a variety of media; about 500 of them are works on paper. See Francis V. O'Connor and Eugene Victor Thaw, *Jackson Pollock: A Catalogue Raisonné of Paintings, Drawings, and Other Works*, vols. 1–4 (New Haven and London: Yale University Press, 1978).

3. Thomas Hart Benton, quoted in Francis V. O'Connor, "The Genesis of Jackson Pollock: 1912 to 1943," *Artforum* 5 (May 1969), p. 17.

4. Krasner, quoted in Friedman, p. 182.

5. The imagery in *War* relates to Picasso's 1937 pair of etchings, *The Dream and Lie of Franco*, and also to his 1937 monumental painting of war, *Guernica*. This information was provided by William S. Lieberman.

6. Jackson Pollock, from a statement titled "My Painting," in *Possibilities I*, no. 1 (New York: Wittenborn Schultz, Winter 1947–48), p. 82.

7. Frank O'Hara, *Jackson Pollock* (New York: George Braziller, 1959), p. 26.

8. See letter of June 7, 1951 from Pollock to Alfonso Ossorio and Ted Dragon, quoted in Friedman, p. 174.

9. Pollock, quoted in Selden Rodman, *Conversations with Artists* (New York: The Devin-Adair Co., 1957), p. 82.

10. Pollock first saw Howell papers used in the collages of Anne Ryan when they were exhibited in 1951 at the Betty Parsons Gallery in a joint show with Lee Krasner's work. After seeing the show, Pollock and Krasner immediately drove to Howell's studio on Long Island and bought about fifty sheets in various colors. See Ellen G. Landau, *Jackson Pollock* (New York: Harry N. Abrams, 1989), pp. 218, 220.

11. Pollock, quoted in "Interview with Jackson Pollock," taped by William Wright, Springs, Long Island, New York, 1950; published in *Art in America* 53, no. 4 (August–September 1965), pp. 111ff.

Richard Pousette-Dart
1916–1992

39. *Undulation Series,* ca. 1941–44
Gouache, watercolor, brush and ink, and
pen and ink on paper
23 × 31½ in. (58.4 × 80 cm)
Gift of Evelyn Pousette-Dart, 1991 (1991.476.1)

40. *Seasons of Light,* ca. 1942–43
Gouache, watercolor, and pen and ink on
paper
22¾ × 31¾ in. (57.8 × 79.4 cm)
Gift of Evelyn Pousette-Dart, 1991 (1991.476.2)

In 1951, Richard Pousette-Dart stated: "The artist must beware of all schools, isms, creeds, or entanglements which would tend to make him other than himself. He must stand alone, free and open in all directions for exits and entrances, and yet with all freedom, he must be solid and real in the substance of his own form."[1] At a three-day symposium held at Studio 35 in New York in April of 1950, during a discussion about naming the Abstract Expressionists in which Pousette-Dart also participated, Willem de Kooning said: "It is disastrous to name ourselves."[2] This individualist stance was shared by all the Abstract Expressionists, even during the formative years of the 1940s, when many of them, including Pousette-Dart, participated in intellectual exchanges and social gatherings.[3] Their camaraderie during that period grew out of their status as outsiders, antiestablishment and artistic nonconformists, and in the 1950s, when their art had matured, most of them stayed to themselves, many spending a considerable amount of their time out of the city. Pousette-Dart was always one of the most intensely private and introspective of the group. By his own assessment, he was not "really close to any of them. . . . I was fiercely by myself and doing my own stuff. I guess I was even belligerent about my aloneness."[4] In 1950, he moved to upstate New York to guard the solitude he cherished; he said that his purpose was to get away from the art world and the commercial element.

Pousette-Dart began painting at the age of eight. He said later about his very early drawings: "I always tended to come at nature through abstraction rather than to come at abstraction through nature."[5] His basic attitudes and intentions were well formulated by the early 1930s, when, in a high-school paper called "Personality in Art," he wrote: "The greater a work of art, the more abstract and impersonal it is, the more it embodies universal experience, and the fewer specific personality traits it reveals."[6] He moved to Manhattan in 1937 and by 1939 was painting full time.

Like the work of his fellow Abstract Expressionists, Pousette-Dart's pictures of the 1940s reflect his intention to convey universal content in abstract terms. His art grew out of his personally based mystical beliefs, exemplified in a statement he wrote in a notebook of ca. 1940: "Art is only significant as it takes us to the whole man and gives us new insights and opens secrets toward the unknown heart of our total mystic awareness."[7] Pousette-Dart was a pacifist, and his opposition to war led him to refuse induction into military service during World War II. This stance is manifested in his art of the early 1940s in a number of pictures that allude to suffering and destruction and to the ultimate power of revelation and regeneration. In the center of *Undulation Series* of ca. 1941–44 (fig. 39), there is a large vertical commanding presence, held at the top by a bulbous horizontal shape, which suggests bones and a cross. This reference to the Crucifixion, symbol of physical and spiritual torment, evokes the continuum of the cycles of death and rebirth, powerfully evident during the war.[8]

The biomorphic and totemic shapes in *Undulation Series* relate this work to contemporaneous pictures of early Abstract Expressionism, as does the underlying irregular grid structure that connects these artists' work of the period to Cubism. Picasso's influence was pervasive, and there may be a relationship here to his *Crucifixion* of 1930, which was exhibited at the Museum of Modern Art in 1939.[9] There are basic similarities in the two works in their overall compositions and in their repetition of circular shapes and use of thin black lines. The early Abstract Expressionist incorporation of Surrealist ideas is also in evidence; Pousette-Dart used automatism as a starting point, as a catalyst to call forth images from his subconscious, and he worked his way through multiple revisions to reach his goal of communicating universal symbols. In a notebook from the early 1940s, the artist

39. *Undulation Series*, ca. 1941–44

wrote: "The accidental in art bores me, high beauty is a conscious moving upon an achievement of pure principle."[10] His contemplative approach most closely relates to his involvement with Far Eastern philosophies and mysticism, an area of influence that also entered into the work of his artistic contemporaries—Robert Motherwell, David Smith, Theodoros Stamos, and Mark Tobey, for instance. Pousette-Dart's belief in the universal consciousness is compatible with the search espoused by his friend John Graham, who, in his influential book titled *System and Dialectics of Art,* wrote that the artist must "re-establish a lost contact with the unconscious...with the primordial racial past...in order to bring to the conscious mind the throbbing events of the unconscious mind."[11]

In *Undulation Series,* the intricate mesh of spontaneous black-and-white lines is held close to the frontal plane by the underlying grid structure. Around the edges of the composition, thin penned squares are visible, and elsewhere, the grid is suggested by the placement of the principal forms, which are vertically and horizontally oriented. In *Seasons of Light* of ca. 1942–43 (fig. 40), the painted white lines of the grid are more clearly visible; the shapes here are round and oval and situated along real or implied diagonal lines. The entire composition vibrates with an allover rhythm and glow. The speckled colors shimmer brightly against the darkened background; they advance and recede within the shallow space. The translucent colored light resembles that of stained-glass windows, a source of inspiration that Pousette-Dart acknowledged in statements and in titles of paintings such as *Amethyst Window* and *Stained Glass.*[12] He equated such light with spiritual enlightenment in one of his many poems:

Art makes opacity luminous
Art makes the unreal real
Art gives to a dark world a luminous internal light.[13]

In the mid-1940s, the artist wrote: "Again and again I approach to unwrap the veils but with all unwrapping I find the form huddled in a formless darkness telling me infinite light is infinite belief."[14] The imagery is swathed in mystical light and flickers as if about to disappear; its meaning is elusive, open-ended, because the mystery it symbolizes is unknowable.

Pousette-Dart was the first Abstract Expressionist to make a mural-size painting, *Symphony Number 1, The Transcendental* of 1941–42, which measures 7½ by 10 feet.[15] At the time it

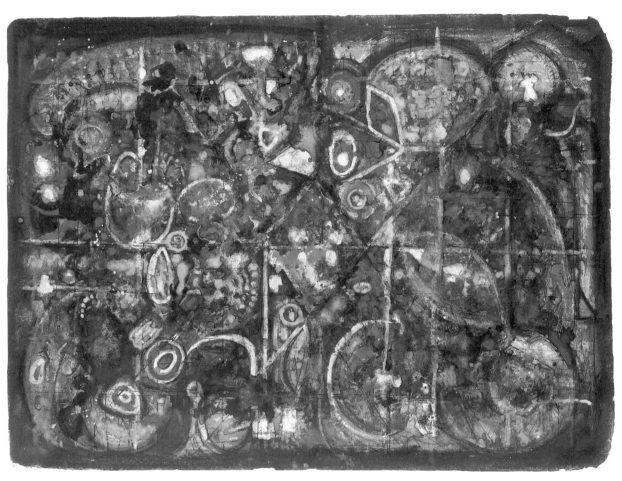

40. *Seasons of Light,* ca. 1942–43

was completed, even Mark Rothko questioned the soundness of making a work so large that it could not easily be shown in a gallery. The imagery in *Seasons of Light* is more abstract and multireferential than that in this large painting, and the media of gouache, watercolor, and ink on paper produced very different effects than those of oil on canvas. The layering of much less viscous media on paper creates a flatter, more translucent surface. As a result of scraping the surface in places with a razor blade, colors are rubbed together and layers underneath are revealed.

Both *Seasons of Light* and *Undulation Series* are independent paintings on paper, displaying the same methods of layering and reworking that characterize Pousette-Dart's canvases. In Pousette-Dart's own words, he always preferred "things of first intensity,"[16] and so, he did not make preliminary sketches for his paintings. In the announcement he wrote for his 1947 exhibition at Art of This Century gallery, the artist set forth the intentions that occupied him consistently from the early 1940s until his death: "I strive to express the spiritual nature of the universe. Painting is for me a dynamic balance and wholeness of life; it is mysterious and transcending, yet solid and real."[17]

1. Richard Pousette-Dart, quoted from a talk at the Boston Museum School, 1951; reprinted in Maurice Tuchman, ed., *New York School: The First Generation* (Greenwich, Connecticut: New York Graphic Society Ltd., n.d.), p. 126.

2. Willem de Kooning, quoted from "Artists' Sessions at Studio 35," April 1950, in Robert Motherwell and Ad Reinhardt, eds., *Modern Artists in America* (New York: Wittenborn Schultz, 1952), p. 22.

3. Pousette-Dart's notebooks record meetings with Rothko, Newman, and Reinhardt over dinner or coffee, conversations with Gottlieb and David Smith, and working on installations of his work at the Betty Parsons Gallery with Newman. He attended the "Subjects of the Artist" school in 1948–49, spoke at the three-day symposium at Studio 35 in 1950, and was in the famous photograph of "The Irascibles" published in *Life* magazine in November 1950.

4. Pousette-Dart, quoted from Rosemary Cohane, *Richard Pousette-Dart: Artistic Sources of an Abstract Style,* master's thesis (Tufts University, 1982), pp. 108–9; reprinted in Judith Higgins, "To the Point of Vision: A Profile of Richard Pousette-Dart," in Sam Hunter, ed., *Transcending Abstraction: Richard Pousette-Dart, Painting 1939–1985,* exh. cat., Fort Lauderdale Museum of Art (Fort Lauderdale, Florida, 1986), p. 19.

5. Pousette-Dart, quoted from Joanne Kuebler, "Concerning Pousette-Dart," Robert Hobbs and Joanne Kuebler, *Richard Pousette-Dart,* exh. cat., Indianapolis Museum of Art (1990), p. 15.

6. Ibid.

7. Ibid., p. 20.

8. Skeletal black-and-white shapes also appeared in 1940s sculptures by Herbert Ferber, David Hare, and Isamu Noguchi. Pousette-Dart sculpted small brass objects, but he did not use skeletal forms in those works.

9. Picasso's *Crucifixion* is in the collection of the Musée Picasso in Paris.

10. Pousette-Dart, quoted from Joanne Kuebler, "Concerning Pousette-Dart," Hobbs and Kuebler, p. 24.

11. John Graham, *System and Dialectics of Art* (New York: Delphic Studios, 1937), p. 33.

12. These titles were listed in the gallery checklist for the exhibition *Richard Pousette-Dart,* Betty Parsons Gallery, New York, March 29–April 17, 1948, nos. 5, 6.

13. Pousette-Dart, quoted from Judith Higgins, "Pousette-Dart's Windows into the Unknowing," *Art News* (January 1987), p. 112.

14. Pousette-Dart, quoted from Kuebler, in Hobbs and Kuebler, p. 85.

15. *Symphony Number 1, The Transcendental,* ca. 1941–42, oil on linen, 90 × 120 in., collection of the artist.

16. Pousette-Dart, quoted from Jerry Tallmer, "The World of Art: One Man Between the Lines," *New York Post,* April 1, 1978, p. 16.

17. Pousette-Dart, quoted from *Richard Pousette-Dart,* exhibition announcement, Art of This Century (New York, 1947), n.p.

Theodore Roszak
1907–1981

41. Study for *Firebird,* 1950

Pen and ink, brush and ink, watercolor,
and pencil on paper

28⅞ × 35 in. (73.3 × 88.9 cm)

The MURIEL KALLIS STEINBERG NEWMAN
COLLECTION, Gift of Muriel Kallis Newman,
in memory of the artist, 1982 (1982.16.2)

Theodore Roszak studied at the School of The Art Institute of Chicago and at the National Academy of Design in New York City during the early to the late 1920s, and he was then working as a painter and lithographer. His skill as a draftsman was already in evidence in 1922–25, in the representational student work he made in Chicago. While on a trip to Europe in 1929, Roszak purchased László Moholy-Nagy's book *New Vision*. Although he did not visit the Bauhaus in Germany, he was thus exposed to Bauhaus-inspired machine art, whose influence is reflected in his drawings from the 1930s. In 1931, he moved permanently to New York City and began to experiment with geometric sculptures and plaster reliefs while he also painted in a similar vein. By 1937, he was producing constructivist sculptures of wood and metal that followed the geo-mechanical thrust of Bauhaus design espoused by Moholy-Nagy, a recent émigré from Europe and the director of the New Bauhaus in Chicago, whom Roszak met in New York in 1938.

From 1940 until his death in 1981, sculpture dominated Roszak's creative output. After World War II, his work changed dramatically, and he began making expressionistic welded-steel sculptures that resemble abstracted prehistoric birds and other monstrous forms. His earlier geometric constructions, based on utopian ideals, no longer seemed appropriate for a world in which war, fueled by new technology, had resulted in so much devastation. In 1952, Roszak noted that his forms became "gnarled and knotted," their surfaces "scorched and coarsely pitted," and that the works are meant "to be blunt reminders of primordial strife and

41. Study for *Firebird*, 1950

struggle, reminiscent of those brute forces that not only produced life but in turn threatened to destroy it."[1] It is these works that place Roszak within the context of Abstract Expressionism. Referring to Roszak, and to sculptors working with related intentions during the 1940s, including Herbert Ferber, David Hare, Ibram Lassaw, Richard Lippold, Seymour Lipton, and David Smith, Ann Gibson wrote: "these sculptors' expressionistic handling in this period, their frequent use of biomorphic forms, and above all, their involvement with content and attitudes similar to those of the Abstract Expressionist painters as seen in their participation in these [artist-run] periodicals makes it appropriate to include them . . . as members of the New York School."[2]

The question of whether Roszak's sculpture, or any other sculpture, can achieve the spontaneity and directness of Abstract Expressionist painting remains at issue,[3] but in the medium of drawing, there is no doubt that Roszak's process and subject matter parallel those of the New York School painters during the postwar years. This common ground is exemplified by a statement Roszak made in 1956: "It is not so much the drawing in the foreground as the drawing that is suggested in the background . . . that . . . is the next sculpture that emerges. . . . It is a self-generating process, by which, through one's own efforts, one tried to scrape the bottom of one's psychic imagination. I find that very often an insignificant part of the drawing, some detail which completely slipped my attention at the moment, gives rise to a very complex set of relationships, and another drawing following subsequently, and after this, another sculpture."[4]

Although chance played a role in his discovery of imagery, Roszak always began his drawings with a specific idea in mind. In his own words, drawing "serves as a means of releasing any number of ideas that could not be so readily recorded in any other media. I know of no other way that one can record one's experiences and impressions so quickly, effectively, and efficiently, than drawing. . . . It acts as an agent by which one can clarify one's thinking and distill many ideas, perhaps even improve on the work itself, by making the mistakes in drawing, so that the drawing becomes a filtering process and a means of selecting ideas, shapes, relationships, and even attitudes."[5] Roszak's drawing methodology changed during the mid-1940s, when his sculpted imagery changed. He no longer sketched the same subject many times on a single sheet, as he had done during the 1930s; instead, he now made one large image at the center of the page and repeated the form in successive drawings to clarify various elements of it. Drawing to work out the forms for his sculptures, Roszak first made small sketches, then larger studies, next full-size drawings, and finally "blueprints" marked with measurements that were used to fabricate the metal sculpture.[6]

Study for *Firebird* of 1950 (fig. 41) is a nearly full-size rendering of the brazed-iron sculpture *Firebird,* which is also in the collection of The Metropolitan Museum of Art.[7] The arching angular form, drawn with spontaneous exuberance, has the directness and energy of gestural Abstract Expressionism. Sweeping thin black-ink lines, nervously scratched on the paper with a pen, define the contours of the single image. These long strokes frequently erupt into turbulent flamelike passages composed of series of short broken curving lines, which mass at the vortex of the form. Out of this central core, which thrusts upward diagonally, many winglike or leglike appendages splay outward in various directions. This relentless allover movement with its attendant feeling of speed is enhanced by the ink spatters that seem to be flying at a high velocity and by the finely drawn halo of parallel lines and cross-hatchings that shimmer around the edges of the form.

The Firebird is a mythic creature from Russian folklore; it was immortalized in the music of the composer Igor Stravinsky in 1910. On hearing this music, Roszak said that he was inspired by the "smoldering chords that accelerate and then whip up into a terrific frenzy of sound."[8] Like the Phoenix, the Firebird rises reborn from the fires of extinction; Roszak spoke of its "emergence out of a complete desolation . . . affirming life."[9] This mythic creature becomes an allusion to the recurrence of the cycles of death and rebirth from ancient times to the post–World War II present. The bird as symbolic of apocalyptic destruction and resurrection appears often in Roszak's work from 1946 to 1951, in *The Scavenger* of 1946–47, *The Spectre of Kitty Hawk* of 1946–47, *Migrant* of 1950, *Skylark* of 1950–51, and *Mandrake* of 1951, for example.[10] The use of myth to convey such meaning through semiabstract forms was prevalent in Abstract Expressionist painting of the 1940s, and the sources for Roszak's work reflect the confluence of ideas that circulated among these painters. He shared their great interest in primitive cultures and in Surrealism, and like many of them, he studied the scientific displays and prehistoric skeletons at New York's Museum of Natural History. Such visual references were accompanied by ideas gleaned from existential philosophy and contemporary literature, for example.

In Study for *Firebird,* the writhing form rises out of a

base that clearly demonstrates its intended transformation into a solid object in three-dimensional space. The spontaneity and energy of the drawing suggest its creation from inner conflict. In the sculpture *Firebird,* the contorted form has solidified, the sensation of anguish made concrete through the tactility of the charred and pitted surface. In both media, Roszak strove to convey an underlying content, which, as he defined it, "bears upon the core structure of an experience and grows from the center out...an orientation of feeling, quality of mood, or direction of an expression."[11]

1. Theodore Roszak, quoted from a symposium titled "The New Sculpture," Museum of Modern Art, 1952; published in Belle Krasne, "A Theodore Roszak Profile," *Art Digest* 27, no. 2 (October 15, 1952), p. 18.

2. Ann Eden Gibson, "Introduction," *Issues in Abstract Expressionism: The Artist-Run Periodicals* (Ann Arbor, Mich.: UMI Research Press, 1990), p. 3.

3. For various opinions, see Mary Delahoyd, "Sculptural Expressions," *Sculptural Expressions: Seven Artists in Metal and Drawing, 1947–1960,* exh. cat., Sarah Lawrence College Gallery (Bronxville, New York, 1985), p. 6; Lisa Phillips, *The Third Dimension: Sculpture of the New York School,* exh. cat., Whitney Museum of American Art (New York, 1984); Stephen Polcari, *Abstract Expressionism and the Modern Experience* (Cambridge University Press, 1991); Carter Ratcliff, "Domesticated Nightmares," *Art in America* (May 1985), pp. 144–51; and Clifford Ross, ed., "Preface," *Abstract Expressionism: Creators and Critics—An Anthology* (New York: Harry N. Abrams, 1990), pp. 11–12.

4. Roszak, quoted from a taped interview with James Elliott, 1956; typescript in Archives of American Art, New York, pp. 37–38.

5. Ibid., p. 36.

6. Krasne, p. 9.

7. Both works were given to the Museum in 1982 by Muriel Kallis Newman. The sculpture measures 31 × 41 × 27 inches (accession number 1982.16.1).

8. Roszak, interview with Elliott, p. 20.

9. Ibid.

10. *The Scavenger,* 1946–47, steel and bronze, 17½ × 16 × 12 in., private collection; *The Spectre of Kitty Hawk,* 1946–47, steel, bronze, and brass, h. 40½ in., Museum of Modern Art, New York; *Migrant,* 1950, steel and copper, h. 28½ in., collection College of Fine and Applied Arts, University of Illinois, Urbana; *Skylark,* 1950–51, steel, h. 99 in., collection Pierre Matisse Gallery, New York; *Mandrake,* 1951, steel and copper, h. 25½ in., Cleveland Museum of Art.

11. Roszak, *In Pursuit of an Image,* no. 2 (Chicago: Time to Time Publications of The Art Institute of Chicago, 1955), p. 10.

Mark Rothko
1903–1970

42. Untitled, ca. 1944–45
Watercolor on paper
30 × 22 in. (76.2 × 55 cm)

Gift of The Mark Rothko Foundation, Inc., 1986
(1986.257.1)

43. Untitled, ca. 1945–46
Watercolor, pen and ink on paper
40½ × 26⅞ in. (102.9 × 68.3 cm)

Gift of The Mark Rothko Foundation, Inc., 1985
(1985.63.8)

44. Untitled, ca. 1945–46
Watercolor, gouache, pen and ink, brush
and ink, and pencil on paper
21¼ × 15¼ in. (54 × 38.7 cm)

Gift of The Mark Rothko Foundation, Inc., 1985
(1985.63.6)

45. Untitled, 1967
Acrylic on paper, mounted on Masonite
29⅞ × 22 in. (75.9 × 55.9 cm)

Gift of The Mark Rothko Foundation, Inc., 1985
(1985.63.1)

46. Untitled, 1967
Acrylic on paper, mounted on Masonite
25¾ × 19¾ in. (65.4 × 50.2 cm)

Gift of The Mark Rothko Foundation, Inc., 1985
(1985.63.2)

Mark Rothko made works on paper in abundance during
only two periods: first, during the mid-1940s, at the beginning of his mature career, when he was searching for an
appropriate means to convey mythic content, and second,

during the late 1960s, near the end of his life, when he was experimenting with new media and then when he became too ill to make large paintings. During the intervening twenty years, Rothko rarely made works on paper, except as sketches for a few commissioned installations.[1]

In 1938, Rothko and his friend Adolph Gottlieb decided to abandon the realistic styles in which they had been working. Rothko stopped painting the genre scenes he had been making since the 1920s and began a series of semiabstract oil paintings of mythic subject matter that continued through the early 1940s. His titles—*Antigone, The Omen, The Syrian Bull,* and *Sacrifice of Iphigenia,* for example—suggest his sources in ancient mythology. By 1943–44, Rothko realized that even this degree of specificity produced a reading that was too limited. As Gottlieb, Barnett Newman, and Rothko wrote in a now-famous 1943 letter to *The New York Times:* "We assert that the subject matter is crucial and only that subject matter is valid which is tragic and timeless. That is why we profess spiritual kinship with primitive and archaic art."[2] Rothko focused primarily on watercolor, a medium whose aqueous nature produces fluid brushstrokes and induces emphasis on generalized forms rather than on details. As Dore Ashton has noted about Rothko's works of this period: "His release from the world of objects occurred as he discovered the delights of watercolor."[3]

Seventy watercolors from the mid-1940s are listed in the Rothko Estate checklist.[4] In these works of ca. 1943–46,[5] large areas of muted color are applied to the paper with soft-bristled brushes in translucent washes. Within these grounds, amorphous shapes are subtly visible. These biomorphic configurations convey a human presence while at the same time alluding to primordial organisms. Vibrating within a shallow space that is demarcated by a ground and/or horizon line, these fragile forms blend into their surroundings, which are composed of combinations of diaphanous grays, browns, and beiges, highlighted and mixed with smaller touches of orange, yellow, blue, green, and red. It has been suggested that the faint coloration of Rothko's backgrounds relates to the ancient Roman frescoes from Boscoreale and Boscotrecase at the Metropolitan Museum, which captured the interest of many of the Abstract Expressionists.[6]

As the three drawings from the mid-1940s in this selection indicate, Rothko was experimenting with a variety of techniques. In his untitled watercolor of ca. 1944–45 (fig. 42), for example, he wiped and scraped away freshly applied paint to expose the lighter stained paper underneath. This was

42. Untitled, ca. 1944–45

usually accomplished with a sharp implement such as a razor blade or the wooden handle of a brush. In some instances, he rubbed with such vigor—note the wiggly passage to the right of center, for example—that he actually wore off the top layer of the paper, a process that left a nubby texture around these areas. In his untitled watercolor and pen and ink of ca. 1945–46 (fig. 43),[7] Rothko spattered and dripped brown paint—a technique he rarely used—over certain sections of the composition, creating a dappled effect. In other works, he diffused the colors by bleeding ink into wet paint. He achieved a golden radiant light through his choice of colors, layering of thin washes, and contrasting of tinted areas with the brightness of the unpainted paper. From photographs of Rothko in his studio, we know that he taped sheets of paper around all four edges to upright wooden boards.[8] The small incidence of drips suggests that he either wiped them away or worked with a controlled amount of watercolor.

The increased freedom of Rothko's experimentation coincided with his increased awareness of European modernist art, including the work of Joan Miró and Paul Klee, both of whom had a considerable impact on many of the Abstract Expressionists. He was also influenced by the Surrealists' use of psychic automatism to create biomorphic images such as those in the paintings and drawings of Matta, Max Ernst, and André Masson. Rothko did not have the direct contact with the Surrealists when they were in America that many of the other Abstract Expressionists had, but he certainly knew their work from exhibitions and publications, and in 1945, he acknowledged their influence on his work of the period.[9] However, he also separated himself from them, writing in 1945, "I love both the object and the dream far too much to have them effervesced into the insubstantiality of memory and hallucination."[10] That same year, Rothko also wrote: "I adhere to the material reality of the world and the substance of things. . . . I insist upon the equal existence of the world engendered in the mind and the world engendered by God outside of it."[11] This statement aligns him more closely with the pantheism of nineteenth-century American landscape painting, and it also hints at his artistic connection with Arthur Dove and Milton Avery, both of whom abstracted directly from nature.

In the relatively large and complex untitled watercolor of ca. 1944–45 (fig. 42),[12] two standing figures appear to be facing two forms in the center of the composition that are surrounded by an aura of light. The totemic beings suggest

43. Untitled, ca. 1945–46

male and female. The one on the right has a hairy ovoid body, a long thick neck, and a jagged roosterlike head that is dominated by a single large eye; the one on the left has delicate fluid lines that form hourglass curves. The two shapes in the center evoke male and female genitalia.[13] Rothko's smaller untitled mixed-media paper of ca. 1945–46 (fig. 44) presents another couple. The figure in the center is large and rotund, with a lollipop head connected by a long line to a bloated torso out of which a long bright-orange phallus protrudes. Once again, the head contains a large circular eye. The figure is set in motion by the sweeping lines of black ink that accentuate its contours. The slender, more graceful feminine form at its left, with arms raised, torso twisting, and one foot thrust forward, seems to be dancing with her partner. Calligraphic black accents and abstract shapes enliven the shallow space, into which the two figures merge. Related imagery and spatial relationships are evident in works of other artists of the period, for example, in Gerome Kamrowski's *Revolve and Devolve* (see fig. 16), in Barnett Newman's *The Song of Orpheus* (see fig. 27), and in Jackson Pollock's untitled drawing of ca. 1945 (see fig. 32).

From his experiments in watercolor, Rothko developed the techniques for his subsequent oil paintings. In his abstract multiform paintings of 1947–50, which immediately followed the watercolors, Rothko diluted the oil paint and brushed it onto the canvas in overlapping layers, and by 1949, he was staining his canvases. The mature works of 1950 to 1970 that follow this brief transitional stage generally consist of two or three brushed irregular rectangular shapes of varying size and color, arranged in horizontal registers on a vertical canvas. Each of these roughly geometric areas hovers on the surface, surrounded by a field of color that creates a halo effect. Diluted paint is stained into the canvas fibers, and the interplay of this translucent surface with the field around it produces what Rothko called the picture's "inner light."[14] These works were not conceived as pure abstractions but as conveyers that, as Rothko said, could express "basic human emotions—tragedy, ecstasy, doom, and so on."[15] In 1952, Rothko explained: "It was not that the figure had been *removed* . . . but the symbols for the figures and in turn the shapes in the later canvases were new *substitutes* for the figures."[16] Rothko sought to create an intimate relationship between the viewer and the painting by literally surrounding him or her with the huge canvas, an idea held in common among the Abstract Expressionists who worked on a monumental scale. The limiting size of working on paper

44. Untitled, ca. 1945–46

made it unsuitable to meet this aim, and between 1947 and 1967, Rothko made only large canvases.

Until 1967, Rothko used oil paints exclusively for his paintings. Perhaps it was as a way of experimenting with acrylic paints that he began making paintings on paper during that year.[17] Because they retained their intense color even when diluted, acrylics could achieve the translucency Rothko desired without sacrificing richness of color. As exemplified by two untitled works of 1967 (figs. 45 and 46), the papers of this period follow the compositional format established in Rothko's paintings of the previous two decades. On their completion, Rothko had these sheets mounted onto Masonite panels so that they, like his paintings, could be hung without frames. Although these pictures cannot compete with the encompassing effect of the large canvases, they exude a monumental quality through the size of the two or three shapes that fill up almost all of the surface. Rothko is reported to have said in 1958: "Small pictures are like tales; large pictures are like dramas."[18]

Bonnie Clearwater has suggested: "The colorful works on paper that date from the latter part of the decade [the 1960s] in particular offered relief to the artist who had lived for years in the constant presence of his dark, nearly monochromatic murals commissioned in 1964 for a chapel in Houston."[19] That project, completed in 1967, is an entire room of black, maroon, and purple paintings. The colors in Rothko's untitled paper of 1967 (see fig. 45) are similar to those in the Houston murals, but the magenta halo around the two dark rectangles in this work on paper gives it a lighter and brighter feeling. Certain properties are unique to the medium of diluted acrylic paints on paper. The artist's brushwork is not very visible, as the paint seeps into the paper in a diffused manner. Also, colors are fused together, in contrast to the unblended colors that result from overlapping layers of oil paint. As opposed to the multiple layers he painted on his canvases, Rothko here applied only a few layers of diluted acrylic, thus controlling the integrity of his colors. The bottom rectangle, of grayish purple, reveals an underlayer of maroon, which can be seen around the ragged edges of the shape. The two dark rectangular shapes stand out from their surrounding field; they are separate entities that nevertheless interact with each other in synchrony to achieve a unified vision.

In the other untitled paper of 1967 in this selection (see fig. 46), the dark brooding colors—reddish brown shapes and midnight-blue field—are very close in tonal value. The

45. Untitled, 1967

three horizontal rectangles are differentiated only by their sizes. The glowing light that enlivens the work discussed above (see fig. 45) is here almost completely obscured. The dulled darkened quality of this work anticipates the further muting of Rothko's palette to the grays and browns that dominate his last works of 1968–69, somber pictures executed primarily on large sheets of paper that followed Rothko's recuperation from an aneurysm of the aorta.

According to the estate list, Rothko produced some eighty-four works on paper during the two years prior to his suicide in February of 1970. This group of sheets was the inspiration for his final series of large, elegiac black-and-gray canvases.

1. Rothko made sketches for the following commissions: Four Seasons restaurant, Seagram Building, New York City, 1958; Holyoke Center, Harvard University, Cambridge, Mass., 1961; and De Menil Chapel, Houston, Texas, 1964.

2. Adolph Gottlieb, Barnett Newman, and Mark Rothko, quoted from their letter of June 7, 1943, published in *The New York Times,* June 13, 1943; reprinted in Bonnie Clearwater, *Mark Rothko: Works on Paper* (New York: Hudson Hills Press, 1984), p. 24.

3. Dore Ashton, "Introduction," Clearwater, p. 10.

4. See checklist of Rothko Estate collection, *The Mark Rothko Foundation: 1976–1986,* 1986, pp. 44–56.

5. Because Rothko did not write dates on his watercolors when he made them, the dates of all of them are approximate. Rothko assigned these works dates in 1968–69, during an inventory of his collection, but since that time, the Rothko Estate has altered the dates in some cases.

6. See Stephen Polcari, *Abstract Expressionism and the Modern Experience* (New York: Cambridge University Press, 1991), pp. 125, 132, 141.

7. This work is one of only six or seven sheets from the period that measures an imposing 27×40 in.

8. The tape is still visible on the Museum's drawings, and there are small holes in the tape, indicating that Rothko tacked these watercolors to backboards.

9. Rothko, quoted from his statement in *Painting Prophecy—1950,* exh. cat., David Porter Gallery (Washington, D.C., 1945); reprinted in Diane Waldman, *Mark Rothko, 1903–1970: A Retrospective,* exh. cat., The Solomon R. Guggenheim Museum (New York, 1978), pp. 48–49.

10. Ibid., p. 49.

11. Rothko, quoted from ibid., p. 48. It has recently been asserted by Anna C. Chave, *Mark Rothko: Subjects in Abstraction* (New Haven: Yale University Press, 1989), that all Rothko's images are founded in reality.

12. This watercolor was signed by Rothko, indicating that it was probably exhibited. Although no exhibition history has been established for the work, Rothko did begin to show his watercolors in New York and elsewhere in 1946.

13. Such references may in part relate to Rothko's courtship at the time of Mary Alice Beistle, called Mel, whom he met in 1944 and married in 1945. The large oil painting *Slow Swirl by the Edge of the Sea,* 1944, $75\frac{1}{8} \times 84\frac{3}{4}$ in., collection the Museum of Modern Art, New York, which has similar figures, has often been interpreted as a double portrait of the couple. Rothko's possible use of personal

46. Untitled, 1967

subjects to convey more universal themes can be related to Arshile Gorky, whose work of the same period has been similarly interpreted; see the essay in this volume on Gorky.

14. Rothko, quoted from his installation instructions for his 1960 retrospective at Whitechapel Art Gallery, London, published in Bonnie Clearwater, "How Rothko Looked at Rothko," *Art News* 84, no. 9 (November, 1985), p. 102.

15. Rothko, quoted from Selden Rodman, *Conversations with Artists* (New York: Capricorn, 1961), pp. 93–94; reprinted in Polcari, p. 144.

16. Rothko, quoted from 1952 interview with William Seitz, cited in Bonnie Clearwater, "Selected Statements by Mark Rothko," in Alan Bowness, *Mark Rothko 1903–1970*, exh. cat., The Tate Gallery (London, 1987), p. 73; reprinted in Polcari, p. 141.

17. Only nine works on paper from 1967 are listed in the Rothko Estate inventory.

18. Rothko, quoted from Dore Ashton, unpublished notes taken at lecture given by Rothko at Pratt Institute, New York, 1958; published in Clearwater, *Mark Rothko: Works on Paper*, p. 37.

19. Clearwater, *Mark Rothko: Works on Paper*, p. 42.

Anne Ryan
1889–1954

47. *Number 319,* 1949
Cut and torn papers, fabrics, gold foil, and
bast fiber pasted on paper, mounted on
black paper
7¾ × 6¾ in. (19.7 × 17.2 cm)

Bequest of Elizabeth McFadden, 1986 (1986.323.7)

48. *Number 30,* 1953
Cut and torn fabrics and papers, pasted on
paper
6⅝ × 5⅞ in. (16.8 × 14.9 cm)

Gift of Elizabeth McFadden, 1956 (56.87.2)

49. *Number 650,* ca. 1953
Cut and torn fabrics, painted papers, gold
foil, and bast fiber, pasted on paper
7 × 7 in. (17.8 × 17.8 cm)

Bequest of Elizabeth McFadden, 1986 (1986.323.13)

50. *Number 547,* 1954
Cut and torn papers and fabrics, pasted on
paper
16¼ × 30 in. (41.3 × 76.2 cm)

Bequest of Elizabeth McFadden, 1986 (1986.323.10)

Several of the Abstract Expressionists made collages. Robert Motherwell made them regularly, Lee Krasner made them
at intervals in between periods when she was painting, and
Willem de Kooning and Franz Kline occasionally incorporated collaged elements into their painted surfaces. Unlike
these artists, who used collage as a secondary medium, Anne
Ryan devoted herself completely to making collages during
the years 1948 to 1954, abandoning the oil painting and print-
making she had been doing since the 1930s. In her collages,
Ryan concentrated for the first time exclusively on the abstract and expressive qualities of shape, line, and color. They

were executed quickly and spontaneously. It has been noted that she produced many compositions in a single day, and her total output over six years numbers about four hundred. In some of these works, the visual effects approximate what the Abstract Expressionists achieved in their drawings and paintings.

Ryan lived and worked in New York City's Greenwich Village, and she was acquainted with several painters and sculptors, many of the New York School—Fritz Bultman, Giorgio Cavallon, Hans Hofmann, Gerome Kamrowski, Barnett Newman, and Tony Smith, for example. During the years 1950 to 1955, she showed at the Betty Parsons Gallery, where several of the Abstract Expressionists also exhibited, and her collages were in several group shows in which they were also included.[1] Although she cannot be called an Abstract Expressionist, Ryan's collages reflect a similar concern for allover imagery in a flat two-dimensional space, an experimental use of media, and a focus on expressive line and fields of color that link her to various manifestations of that movement. In formal terms, one can compare Ryan's collages with the other works on paper in this selection.

In other important areas, however, her work differs from theirs. Ryan had no apparent concern for a philosophical agenda; no primitive or universal content was at the root of her intentions; no dramatic struggle to divine humanity's place in the universe guided her work. Rather, her collages are intensely private and poetic contemplations, fragile and intimate and very much the opposite of the Abstract Expressionist heroic sublime. These differences are directly manifested in the small scale of Ryan's works. During the same years that artists such as Robert Motherwell, Barnett Newman, Jackson Pollock, and Mark Rothko, for example, were working on wall-sized canvases that envelop the viewer, Ryan persistently created an oeuvre of small proportions that sought intimacy with the viewer, but in a completely different way. Her pieces rarely exceeded seven by eight inches in measurement, the only exception being a group of larger collages of 1952–54, some of which are about four feet in length. Such small works force the viewer to focus in close-up in order to perceive the subtleties of the composition. The possibility of increasing her scale was broached to Ryan in the fall of 1951 by Newman and Tony Smith at the instigation of Rothko, who had just seen her work at Betty Parsons.[2] Ryan totally rebuked their suggestion, although a few years later, she did experiment with enlarging her format somewhat.

47. *Number 319*, 1949

Ryan came to the collage medium late in life, in 1948, when she was fifty-eight. Since 1925, she had been earning a meager living as a writer, and her poetry, novels, short stories, biography, and newspaper articles continued to be published until her death in 1954. After 1941, she began to show her prints and paintings in several one-person and group exhibitions, but she had not yet found the métier that could be a visual corollary for her poetic nature. This occurrence took place in January of 1948, when Ryan visited a memorial exhibition of the collages of Kurt Schwitters at Pincotheca-Rose Fried Gallery. After viewing the show in "a passion of delight,"[3] Ryan went home to make her own collaged impressions. Over the next few weeks, she went back to the gallery three more times to study Schwitters's collages. Her early collages that followed emulated his works; they are dense geometric compositions that incorporate "found" papers such as postage stamps, printed papers, and photographs that have some connotative significance. Shortly thereafter, Ryan began to develop her own style, which eliminated all narrative references in favor of complete abstraction.

Ryan's collages are characterized by their subtle interplay of various textures and their careful orchestration of limited tonal ranges. The four pieces in this selection demonstrate the nuances within each work and the interrelationships and variations that occur from work to work. For example, the colors in *Number 30* (fig. 48) are muted and monochromatic, while in *Number 319* (fig. 47), black plays a key role, acting as the border color and as some of the shapes and linear elements. In *Number 30* and *Number 547* (fig. 50), the emphasis is on distinctive geometric shapes that hover in a colored ground, while in *Number 319* and *Number 650* (fig. 49), the dense overlapping irregular shapes and linear accents create an allover composition in which form, line, and ground are inextricably meshed together. In these four works, there are reminders of Abstract Expressionism—in *Number 30* and *Number 547,* of Rothko's hovering rectangles, and in *Number 319* and *Number 650,* of Pollock's linear skeins.

To make her collages, Ryan collected delicate sheer gauze and netting, pieces of textured and patterned silk and satin, bits of gold foil, Chinese tea papers, thin rice papers, and Douglass Howell's handmade rag papers that she had seen while working at Atelier 17, Stanley William Hayter's print studio in New York. At first, she mounted her collages onto square or oval sheets of Howell paper, but soon, these papers became a primary element in her collaged surfaces. At one point, she even took some of Howell's raw materials

48. *Number 30*, 1953

from his studio before they were processed and incorporated them into her works. The fabrics Ryan used were carefully chosen for their tactile qualities. The more shredded and worn they were, the better she liked them. Her daughter has recalled that "when something in the house got old, acquired by wear a 'feel,' and to the usual person was ready for the trash can, then we would say, 'Now it's getting to the collage stage.'"[4] These pieces of cloth were sorted and kept near Ryan's large worktable in old shoe boxes that were labeled by color. Many different collages include pieces of the same fabric, creating a visual unity among the works.

Although most of Ryan's collages have been inventoried, there is still difficulty in determining their exact sequence and dating. Most are signed, but few are dated, and even her numbered titles are of little help, since there are so many gaps and repetitions. In addition, no major stylistic changes took place that might indicate a particular sequence. The changes that are perceptible are general ones—between the Schwitters-inspired collages and her subsequent abstractions, and between the small works and the late larger ones. Over the six years during which Ryan produced collages, her compositions alternated between animated, complex allover patterns and quiet, more simplified fields of color divided by small squares. As *Number 30* and *Number 650* demonstrate, these two formats occur simultaneously.

Number 547, one of Ryan's last works, has the unusual distinction of being signed with her full name and dated. Like many of Ryan's late works, this one is considerably larger than her earlier characteristic scale, suggesting that during the last two years of her life, she may have begun to respond to the Abstract Expressionists' enormous canvases of the early 1950s. In *Number 547,* Ryan had the physical space in which to develop a more complex composition with several motifs, and she used it effectively to engage large and small elements in a lively dialogue. The muted ground is made of pieces of white, beige, and gray-blue papers and fabrics that are several inches square, larger than the elements Ryan used in her smaller works. Also unlike the earlier gridlike collages, the squares in *Number 547* are oriented on a diagonal that moves the eye across the field in a rolling motion, which is amplified by subtle changes in texture and variations in color. With playful humor, the artist juxtaposed small squares and slightly larger triangles of bright orange, yellow-orange, rust, and cordovan. These shapes and the seven thin vertical stripes that anchor the horizontal movement create the impression

49. *Number 650,* ca. 1953

of shallow depth, as they are clearly positioned in the fore-front against the lighter background. This slightly three-dimensional space is atypical of Ryan; even when pieces of paper or fabric overlap, there is little or no sense of depth in Ryan's collages.

Although her public reputation has always been a modest one, Ryan's contribution to expanding the expressive potential of the collage medium has been acknowledged within the art world. The formal connections between her collages and the works of the Abstract Expressionists, however, have rarely been discussed. Concerning that issue, Deborah Solomon summarized some areas of convergence and divergence in a recent article: "There is something of Ad Reinhardt in her [Ryan's] reverence for the rectangle, and something of Rothko in the soft luminosity of her colors. There are intimations of Bradley Walker Tomlin in the tight, constrained rhythms of her 'allover' compositions. . . . clearly she was sympathetic to their work. . . . she responded with speed and flair to the most radical developments of her time. On the other hand, one doesn't want to make too much of her connection to Abstract Expressionism. . . . Her basic allegiance was to European abstraction as opposed to its American variations."[5]

1. Anne Ryan's collages were shown four times at the Betty Parsons Gallery: in 1950, 1951 (with Lee Krasner's paintings), 1954, and 1955 (memorial exhibition). In 1951, one of her collages was included in the Museum of Modern Art's exhibition "Abstract Painting and Sculpture in America" and was illustrated alongside paintings by Motherwell, Reinhardt, and Tomlin. Later that same year, Ryan participated in the "9th Street: Exhibition of Paintings and Sculpture," held at a storefront gallery in New York City; also in that show were James Brooks, Elaine and Willem de Kooning, Philip Guston, Franz Kline, Lee Krasner, Robert Motherwell, Jackson Pollock, Richard Pousette-Dart, Theodoros Stamos, and Bradley Walker Tomlin.

2. Ryan's work was installed at the Betty Parsons Gallery in 1951 in a two-person show with Lee Krasner. The details of Ryan's meeting with Barnett Newman and Tony Smith are told in Elizabeth McFadden, "Anne Ryan: A Personal Remembrance" (unpublished manuscript, ca. 1982–83), p. 239, in archives of the Department of 20th Century Art, The Metropolitan Museum of Art.

3. Elizabeth McFadden, quoted from Sarah Faunce, *Anne Ryan: Collages*, exh. cat., The Brooklyn Museum (1974), p. 7.

4. Elizabeth Eaton McFadden, "Anne Ryan," *The Saint Elizabeth Alumna* (Spring 1956), p. 2.

5. Deborah Solomon, "Art: The Hidden Legacy of Anne Ryan," *The New Criterion* (New York: January 1989), p. 55.

50. *Number 547*, 1954

David Smith
1906–1965

51. ΔΣ *32–12–57*, 1957
Brush and ink with egg on paper
17 × 22 in. (43.2 × 55.9 cm)
Anonymous Gift, 1978 (1978.567.3)

Critics and scholars of the period have unanimously agreed that Abstract Expressionism is the province of painters. Arguments have been advanced for the inclusion of a number of sculptors, including Herbert Ferber, David Hare, Ibram Lassaw, Richard Lippold, Seymour Lipton, Theodore Roszak, and David Smith. There is general agreement in the case of only one, David Smith, whose ideas and work most closely correspond to those of the major painters of the Abstract Expressionist movement.

Smith was initially trained as a painter in New York City from the late 1920s to the early 1930s. Even after he turned to sculpture in 1931, he continued to paint and to associate with painters, a number of whom became major figures in Abstract Expressionism—Arshile Gorky, Adolph Gottlieb, Willem de Kooning, Robert Motherwell, and Jackson Pollock, for example. In 1961, Smith noted: "I belong with painters, in a sense; and all my early friends were painters because we all studied together. And I never conceived of myself as anything other than a painter because my work came right through the raised surface, and color and objects applied to the surface."[1] Smith's kinship with the ideas of the Abstract Expressionist painters is reflected in his 1953 statement, in which he defined sculpture as the representation of energy: " . . . the indication of form by bulk mass does not possess its old validity. Mass is energy. Space is energy. Nothing is without energy. Nothing is without mass. The indication of area or pattern is a statement of energy and as sculptural as sculpture can be."[2] Like the Abstract Expressionist painters, Smith proclaimed the artist's freedom to create forms spontaneously through the making process and to work with unleashed, and often aggressive, intensity. Also like them, Smith believed in the artist's self-identification with the work of art. Smith expounded on this intimate relationship between

51. ΔΣ *32-12-57*, 1957

the artist and his work: "I never intend a day to pass without asserting my identity; my work records my existence."³

Smith placed a premium on sustaining "the original creative impulse."⁴ He once remarked that he wanted "to make sculpture as free as drawing."⁵ In his welded-steel works, Smith used a technique that allowed for maximum flexibility. However, it still took him long hours to cut, arrange, and weld each piece. No such delay exists between the creative impulse and the act of drawing, which allows the artist to record his emotions immediately and directly. Smith was a prolific draftsman, and he drew nearly every day. Drawing was central to his creative process. In fact, he regarded it as "the life force of the Artist."⁶ He saw drawing as "the most direct, closest to the true self. . . . It may have been the first celebration of man with his secret self—even before song."⁷ Smith said of his drawings that they "are studies for sculpture, sometimes what sculpture is, sometimes what sculptures can never be. Sometimes they are atmospheres from which sculptural form is unconsciously selected during the labor process of producing form. Then again they may be amorphous floating direct statements in which I am the subject, and the drawing is the act."⁸

Smith's sculpture, which relied more heavily on line and shape than it did on mass and depth, has been described as "drawing in the air"; it is more closely associated with painting and drawing than any earlier sculpture in the history of art. Smith's description of his working method—which directly corresponds to that of the Abstract Expressionist painters—points out the essential role of drawing in his development of a radical new idea of sculpture: "I follow no set procedure in starting a sculpture. Some works start out as chalk drawings on the cement floor with cut steel forms working into the drawings. When it reaches the stage when the structure can become united, it is welded into position upright. Then the added dimension requires different considerations over the more or less profile form of the floor drawing assembly. Sometimes I make a lot of drawings using possibly one relationship in each drawing which will add up in the final work. Sometimes sculptures just start with no drawing at all."⁹

Drawing served several different functions for Smith. Between the late 1930s and the early 1950s, he filled over forty sketchbooks with ideas for new sculpture and analytical records of works already completed. By the mid-1950s and into the 1960s, he was drawing less in sketchbooks, producing instead hundreds of larger independent works on paper, primarily in brush and ink. These were drawn in his house studio, which contained cabinets for work, drawing stock and tables, an etching press, and record photographs. He stood at a table set before a window, and he was surrounded by his paints and inks, with a stack of paper nearby. The type of paper varied from high-quality linen rag paper to standard drawing stock. Smith mixed them together in a pile so that he could work freely. As he finished a drawing, he often dropped the wet sheet of paper onto the floor.

During the years 1957 and 1958, Smith produced over four hundred drawings. The Metropolitan's *ΔΣ 32–12–57*[10] (fig. 51) is a fine example of a group of large calligraphic brush-and-ink works on paper that demonstrate the dynamic brushstrokes that also characterize the works of the gestural painters of the period. Using the unusual medium of Chinese ink mixed with egg yolk that he devised in 1953, Smith produced a viscous liquid that is fairly opaque and matte in appearance. As the ink was applied with a brush, the bristles left textured streaks within the ink that reveal the various nuances of the artist's touch. Each stroke is perceived separately, even when strokes overlap. This phenomenon produces a clear delineation of the different overlapping planes. The drawn image is therefore not just a collection of flat marks on a two-dimensional plane; it is also an allusory reference to the three-dimensional world. In his stainless-steel sculptures of the 1960s, Smith created a similar allusion to three-dimensional space on a flat surface by "drawing" on the metal skeins of burnished lines that reflect the light. In *ΔΣ 32–12–57*, Smith created larger multifaceted forms with a series of individual dabs and dashes of ink, using a process that relates to his approach to making sculpture—typically from multiple pieces of metal that he cut to size and arranged on the floor before welding. This additive process of creating a unified image from a number of components was, as Smith noted, "conceptually...much like painting. The sculptural entity never takes place until summed up by its parts."[11]

In an extension of this idea, the overall composition of *ΔΣ 32–12–57* is also a joining together of separate units, and the blank space between them acts as an integral part of the work. When Smith installed his sculptures on his property in Bolton Landing in upstate New York, he carefully orchestrated their juxtapositions to create groupings that could be seen as a unit, with the open spaces between acting as positive elements in the overall image. Smith sometimes arranged groupings of smaller works on the dock at Bolton Landing, and the photographs he took of these show that he often placed three sculptures in a row. As seen in ΔΣ *32–12–57* and also in several other drawings, it is a format that Smith frequently repeated on paper.

Abstract shapes that allude to human form are common in Smith's drawings, paintings, and sculptures, as exemplified in ΔΣ *32–12–57,* in which the energetic movement of three humanoid figures is conveyed by the gestural brushstrokes. Such drawings frequently have been compared with Chinese and Japanese painting and calligraphy, and there is a similarity in process and in the emotive content conveyed by the graphic markings themselves. More important, however, is Smith's affinity with the Eastern idea of the artist's self-identification with nature and with the work of art, a connection avowed by many of the Abstract Expressionist painters. For Smith, whether the drawing was to lead directly to a sculptural form or not, it was always an expression of self, a celebration of the artist's freedom and a visualization of his Abstract Expressionist intention to find subject matter of universal significance in abstract form. Smith and Jackson Pollock, two of the major innovators of the group, fulfilled this goal via their radical redefinitions of drawing, Pollock with paint on canvas and Smith—informed by the unique vision of the sculptor—with welded steel.

1. David Smith in 1961, quoted from Trinkett Clark, *The Drawings of David Smith,* exh. cat., International Exhibitions Foundation (Washington, D.C., 1985), p. 18.

2. Smith in 1953, quoted from *David Smith by David Smith,* ed. Cleve Gray (London: Thames and Hudson, 1968), p. 54.

3. Smith in 1953, quoted from Paul Cummings, *David Smith, The Drawings,* exh. cat., Whitney Museum of American Art (New York, 1979), p. 21.

4. Smith in 1955, quoted from *David Smith,* ed. Garnett McCoy (New York: Praeger Publishers, 1973), p. 137.

5. Ibid.

6. Smith in 1955, quoted from Gray, p. 84.

7. Ibid.

8. Ibid., p. 104.

9. Ibid., p. 55.

10. Smith began to sign some of his works with the Greek letters ΔΣ (delta, sigma) in the 1930s. In this paper, the number 32 refers to the work's place in a series; 12 and 57 refer to the month and the year executed respectively.

11. Smith in 1953, quoted from Gray, p. 54.

Theodoros Stamos
Born 1922

52. Untitled, 1947

Watercolor, brush and ink, pastel, and gouache on paper

20 × 26 in. (50.8 × 66 cm)

Anonymous Gift, in memory of Mr. and Mrs. Theodoros Stamatelos, 1991 (1991.41.4)

53. Untitled, 1947

Watercolor, brush and ink, pastel, and gouache on paper

20 × 26 in. (50.8 × 66 cm)

Anonymous Gift, in memory of Mr. and Mrs. Theodoros Stamatelos, 1991 (1991.41.5)

54. Study for *Hibernation*, 1947

Watercolor, pen and ink, and gouache on paper

11½ × 20 in. (29.2 × 50.8 cm)

Anonymous Gift, in memory of Mr. and Mrs. Theodoros Stamatelos, 1991 (1991.41.2)

55. *Partitions*, 1947

Watercolor, gouache, pen and ink, and brush and ink on paper

16 × 12 in. (40.6 × 30.5 cm)

Anonymous Gift, in memory of Mr. and Mrs. Theodoros Stamatelos, 1991 (1991.41.3)

By 1947, the year that Theodoros Stamos made the four works on paper in this selection, he had already achieved a considerable amount of success for an artist who was not yet twenty-five years old. Between 1943 and 1947, this youngest first-generation Abstract Expressionist was given three one-person exhibitions in New York City, was included in several group shows—including the Whitney Museum of

American Art's annual exhibitions of contemporary American painting and the important showing of early Abstract Expressionist works titled "The Ideographic Picture" assembled by Barnett Newman at the Betty Parsons Gallery—and had his pictures acquired by the Museum of Modern Art in New York and by the private collector Edward W. Root, who eventually owned thirty-two of his works.[1]

Stamos is completely self-taught as a painter. He started working at home in 1937, and his earliest pictures are primitive landscapes and imagined scenes of Greece based on stories told to him by his mother about her homeland. In 1943, at the time of his first exhibition at Betty Parsons's Wakefield Gallery and Book Store in Manhattan, Stamos met Adolph Gottlieb and Barnett Newman. The two older artists recognized Stamos's natural abilities as a painter and saw a parallel between Stamos's subject matter and their own idea of using primitive and mythological imagery, which they set forth, with Mark Rothko, in their letter of June 9, 1943 to *The New York Times*.[2] Over the next few years, Newman was particularly supportive of Stamos's work; he wrote an eloquent introductory essay for Stamos's one-person exhibition at the Betty Parsons Gallery, which was held from February 10 to March 1, 1947. It was, however, with Rothko that Stamos maintained the closest friendship, which lasted from 1947 until Rothko's death in 1970. Even before they met around 1945–46, these two artists were producing similar imagery, and although their work has always been distinctively individualistic, their kinship was based on their closely related artistic sensibilities.

Like Newman and Rothko, Stamos explored organic forms and ancient mythology in his pictures of the mid- to late 1940s, which were meant to suggest the interconnections among all levels of nature and the continuity between the primordial past and the present. In his introduction to Stamos's 1947 exhibition, Newman characterizes his fellow-artist's work incisively, pointing out Stamos's individual contribution to the collectively held ideas of the early Abstract Expressionists: "The work of Theodoros Stamos, subtle and sensuous as it is, reveals an attitude toward nature that is closer to true communion. His ideographs capture the moment of totemic affinity with the rock and the mushroom, the crayfish and the seaweed. He redefines the pastoral experience as one of participation with the inner life of the natural phenomenon. One might say that instead of going to the rock, he comes out of it. In this Stamos is on the same

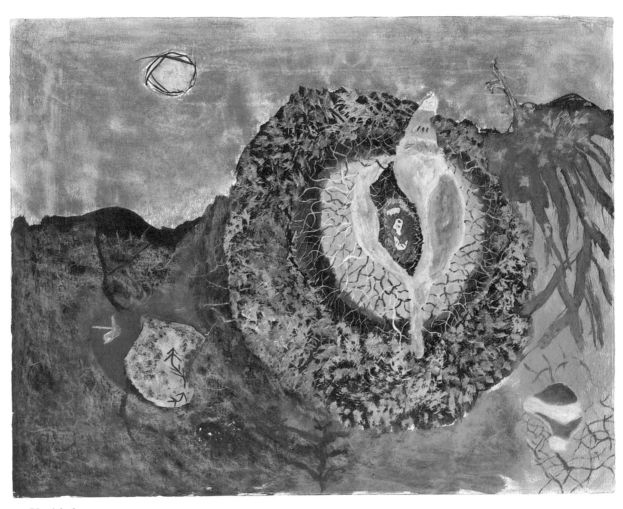

52. Untitled, 1947

fundamental ground as the primitive artist who never portrayed the phenomenon as an object of romance and sentiment, but always as an expression of the original noumenistic mystery in which rock and man are equal."[3]

From the early 1940s to the present, Stamos has always found endless wonder in the mysteries of nature and its phenomena. During the 1940s, he often visited the American Museum of Natural History, where he saw the displays of fossils and gems. He also collected numerous books on the natural sciences, including botany, geology, mineralogy, and oceanography, and the detailed illustrations in these volumes were a fertile source of inspiration. Stamos was fascinated by Charles Darwin, whose ideas he studied in books such as *The Power of Movement in Plants,* after which he titled a picture in 1945.[4] References to a number of forms from nature are evident in Stamos's untitled of 1947 (fig. 52). The space is divided by an undulating horizon line that is visible on the left third of the picture; a small yellow-orange orb hovers above it, like the sun wavering in an overcast sky. In the center of the ground, a large, roughly round rocklike form extends upward into the gray expanse. Its outer layer is connected to its yellow-green core by a profusion of delicate white lines that suggest cracks caused by some kind of turbulence. A conchshell shape breaks through from within the core. The division of the lower portion of the composition into green on the left and blue on the right and the placement of the rock-and-shell form strongly evoke the shore. Teeming with life and growth, the whole scene recalls the activities of nature's secret regions. This somehow familiar yet mysterious place conveys the intentions expressed by Stamos in a statement he made in December of 1947: "I am concerned with the Ancestral Image which is a journey through the shells and webbed entanglements of the phenomenon. At the end of such a journey is the impulse of remembrance and the picture created is the embodiment of the Ancestral World that exists on the horizon of mind and coast."[5]

In a lecture he wrote and delivered in 1954 titled "Why Nature in Art," Stamos spoke poetically about Chinese and Japanese art and their relevance for the contemporary artist. His interest in Eastern art, philosophy, and poetry began in the mid-1940s and was further advanced by his friendship with the poet Robert Price, who had also developed an affinity with these sources. Stamos met Price in 1946, while they

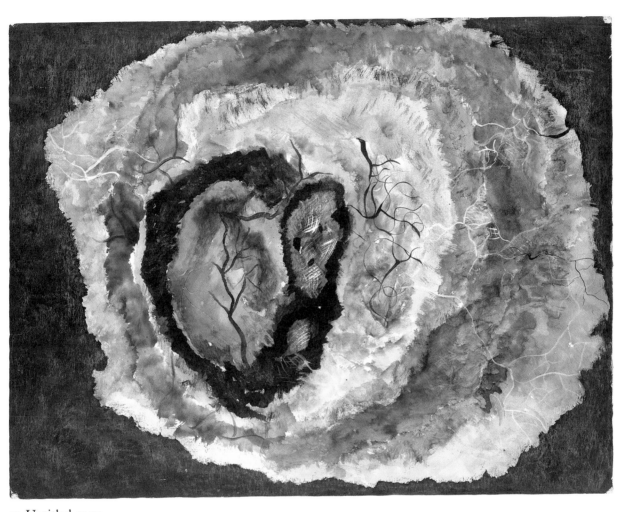

53. Untitled, 1947

were both working on an issue of the *Tiger's Eye,* an important magazine in the history of early Abstract Expressionism that combined visual art with literature, and until his untimely death in 1954, Price was a guiding spirit for Stamos's art. During the 1940s, Stamos collected many books on Asian art and literature, and he visited the Freer Gallery in Washington, D.C., where he saw the renowned collection of Japanese art and also the Japanese-inspired works of the nineteenth-century American James McNeill Whistler. Other Abstract Expressionists—Robert Motherwell, Richard Pousette-Dart, David Smith, and Clyfford Still, for example—also found an affinity with the Eastern concept of humanity's oneness with universal nature.

In "Why Nature in Art," Stamos allied Eastern art and ideas with the pantheism of nineteenth-century American landscape painters and with the early-twentieth-century modernist painter Arthur Dove, who worked prolifically on paper. Referring to Dove's pictures from after 1930, Stamos said that they are "more organic, with color patterns related to flames and amorphous growths of the woods... beautiful compositions that at times resemble the expressive glory of Chinese calligraphic characters while never deviating from their base in a physical world."[6] Stamos knew and admired Dove's work from the late 1930s, when he saw it on many visits to Alfred Stieglitz's gallery. Dove's influence, openly avowed by Stamos, is visible in his works of the mid-1940s, in untitled of 1947 (fig. 53), for example, in which the single, light-filled cocoonlike form of concentric circles particularly recalls the earlier twentieth-century American. Stamos's form, however, differs from Dove's abstractions of the outer elements of nature in its darker, more brooding evocation of secret inner realms.

During the spring of 1947, Stamos traveled by train through New Mexico, California, and Washington State. He had been interested in the works of Morris Graves and Mark Tobey since the early 1940s, when he first saw them in New York galleries, and during his trip west, he sought out these two artists, actually meeting Tobey and unfortunately missing Graves. The rugged landscape along his route inspired numerous works on paper. The four watercolors in this selection exemplify Stamos's use of mottled, scumbled, and patterned surfaces that convey the rough, timeworn textures of rocks and weather-beaten earth. As Stamos wrote of such pictures in 1957, "Textures and brittle, feathery surfaces became an obsession."[7]

54. Study for *Hibernation*, 1947

Watercolor on paper was an important medium for Stamos in the development of his oil paintings on Masonite of the same period. Washes of watercolor naturally create translucent surfaces and mottled effects, and Stamos greatly diluted his oils to achieve similarly textured surfaces. A comparison of Study for *Hibernation* of 1947 (fig. 54) with Stamos's oil-on-Masonite *Hibernation* of the same year[8] is specifically enlightening in this regard. Like all Stamos's works on paper, it was executed as an independent work of art that could stand on its own, as is attested by the fact that it was Stamos's only entry in the *Abstract and Surrealist American Art* exhibition at the Art Institute of Chicago that opened in November of 1947.[9] This work was chosen by the artist as an image he could use as the basis for an oil on Masonite. In the watercolor, the two large forms—one resembling a fossilized rock-skull and the other a shell-shaped leaflike torso—fill the entire surface and seem about to burst out of the space of the elongated piece of paper, which was torn from a larger sheet. In the oil, the roughly similar shapes exist in a more open, less confining space.

Hints of Stamos's impending move further into abstraction are evident in *Partitions* of 1947 (fig. 55), in which broad areas of mottled earth-and-sea tones interlock. The large tripartite form in the center suggests fissured rock, leaves, and shells, while the darkly outlined shape at the lower left resembles an animal skull with one eye. Beginning in the late 1940s, Stamos's works became larger and more abstract. During the 1950s and 1960s, he was completely occupied by large canvases and made few works on paper. Starting with his *Infinity Field* series of the 1970s and continuing to the present, Stamos has been making numerous paintings on paper regularly, and these, like his works on paper of the 1940s, are both independent statements and fertile inspirations for his larger canvases.

1. These thirty-two pictures are now in the Munson-Williams-Proctor Institute, Utica, New York; Edward W. Root Bequest.

2. For more information about this letter, see the essays in this volume on Gottlieb and Rothko.

3. Barnett Newman, quoted from his introductory essay for the exhibition brochure, "Stamos," Betty Parsons Gallery, New York, 1947; reprinted in John P. O'Neill, ed., *Barnett Newman: Selected Writings and Interviews* (New York: Alfred A. Knopf, 1990), pp. 109–10.

4. The picture Stamos made is titled *Movement of Plants*, 1945, oil on Masonite, 16×20 in., Munson-Williams-Proctor Institute, Utica, New York; Edward W.

55. *Partitions,* 1947

Root Bequest. It was exhibited in the Whitney Museum of American Art's Annual Exhibition in 1945 and was the first of thirty-two Stamos pictures purchased by Root.

5. Stamos, his statement from "The Ides of Art: The Attitudes of 10 Artists on their Art and Contemporaneousness," *Tiger's Eye* 1, no. 2 (December 1947), p. 43.

6. Stamos, quoted from his 1954 lecture "Why Nature in Art"; published in Barbara Cavaliere, "Theodoros Stamos in Perspective," *Arts Magazine* 52, no. 4 (December 1977), p. 105.

7. Stamos, quoted from his answers to a 1957 Whitney Museum of American Art questionnaire; reprinted in Cavaliere, p. 105.

8. *Hibernation,* 1947, oil on Masonite, 24 × 30 in., collection Addison Gallery of American Art, Addison, Ma., is one of the thirty-two works by Stamos purchased by Edward W. Root.

9. See checklist of the exhibition, *Abstract and Surrealist American Art*, exh. cat., Art Institute of Chicago (1947).

Mark Tobey
1890–1976

56. *Blaze of our Century,* 1947
Tempera on paper
26 × 19⅞ in. (66 × 50.5 cm)

From the Collection of Dr. and Mrs. Samuel
Ernest Sussman, Bequest of Blanche Risa Sussman,
1990 (1991.129.2a,b)

57. *Transit,* 1948
Tempera, brush and ink, wash, and chalk
on paper
24½ × 19 in. (62.2 × 48.3 cm)

George A. Hearn Fund, 1949 (49.160.1)

58. *Autumn Field,* 1955
Tempera on paper
20⅞ × 35¾ in. (53 × 90.8 cm)

From the Collection of Dr. and Mrs. Samuel
Ernest Sussman, Bequest of Blanche Risa Sussman,
1990 (1991.129.3)

59. *World Dust,* 1957
Gouache and watercolor on paper
37 × 25 in. (94 × 63.5 cm)

Arthur Hoppock Hearn Fund, 1958 (58.25)

60. Untitled, 1957
Brush and ink on paper
13¼ × 9⅝ in. (33.7 × 24.5 cm)

Gift of Dr. and Mrs. Hyman G. Weitzen, 1981
(1981.490.2)

Mark Tobey is recognized as an artist who exerted an influence
on the Abstract Expressionist painters who emerged in New
York City during the 1940s. During most of that period, he

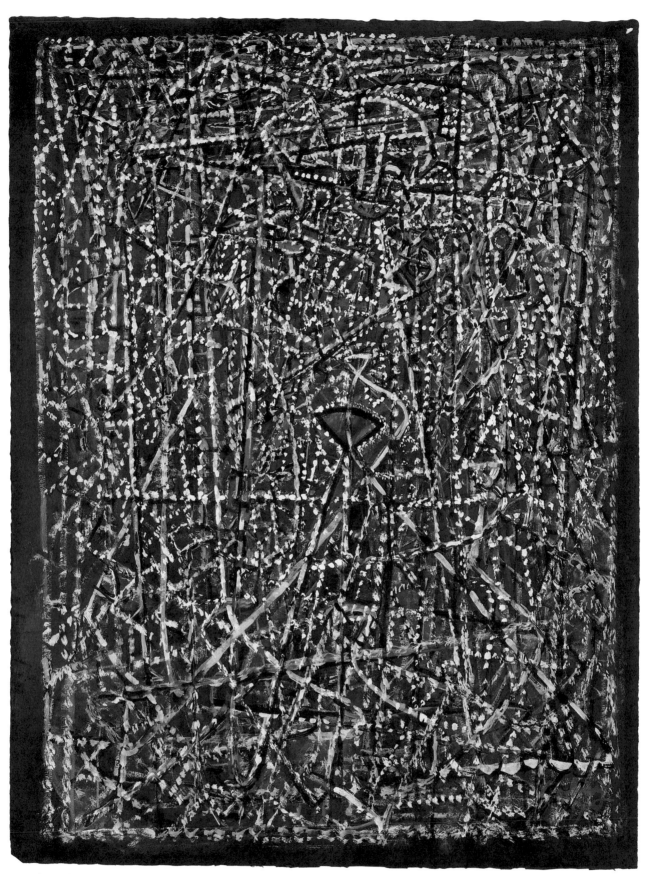

56. *Blaze of our Century*, 1947

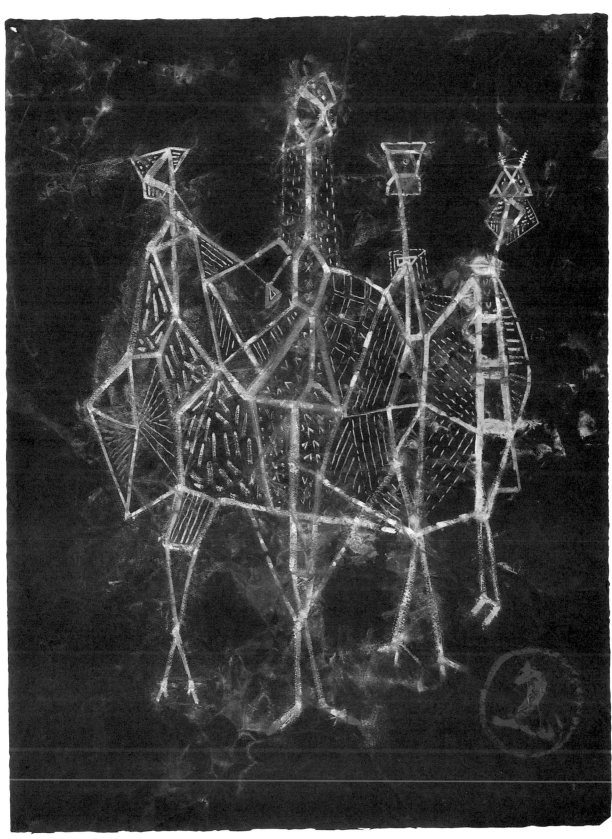

56a. *Blaze of our Century,* 1947 (verso)

lived in Seattle, with short stays in Europe, and he was therefore not directly involved in the development of the New York School. From 1942 to 1955, his work was included in more than twenty-five exhibitions in New York, and it was well known to the Abstract Expressionists.[1] Tobey was a regular visitor to New York City, where he often spent several months at a time, particularly during the 1950s.

Until the mid-1930s, Tobey made realistic depictions of people and places. In 1935–36, he began evolving an abstract style composed of a network of energetically painted white lines in which recognizable shapes appear at intervals from within the mesh. Although these lines appear fluid and lyrical, they were executed with a controlled and studied motion. During the 1940s, Tobey's so-called "white writing" moved further into abstraction. Beginning in that period and continuing throughout the rest of his life, Tobey created works in which allover linear motions articulate a deep three-dimensional space filled with light and rhythm that suggest cosmic realms. They are intricate environments in which "the idea is to achieve an equilibrium."[2] While Tobey occasionally used oil paint on canvas, his primary medium was tempera, gouache, or ink on paper. Because of his choice of support, the majority of his oeuvre is small in scale compared with the much larger paintings of the Abstract Expressionists.

Tobey's titles are referential but nonspecific; often they are metaphors for spiritual states of being. They leave subject matter open to various possible interpretations. In *Blaze of our Century* of 1947 (fig. 56), for example, the myriad of white dots that cover the entire sheet of black paper creates a flickering atmosphere that evokes the lights that illumine contemporary urban centers and also suggests the blaze of destruction that resulted from World War II.[3] Several schematized figures are visible from within the surface, one with bright red lips. They are like ghostly apparitions, perhaps forms in the urban night or reminders of the many lives lost in the war.[4] Tobey's completely abstract *World Dust* (fig. 59), made ten years later, in 1957, also hints at apocalyptic events, and it exemplifies Tobey's intention to express the interconnectedness of the microcosm and the macrocosm. In the artist's own words: "My sources of inspiration have gone from those of my native Middle West to those of microscopic worlds. I have discovered many a universe on paving stones and tree barks."[5]

Tobey's artistic development is directly connected to his commitment to the Bahá'í World Faith, which he joined in

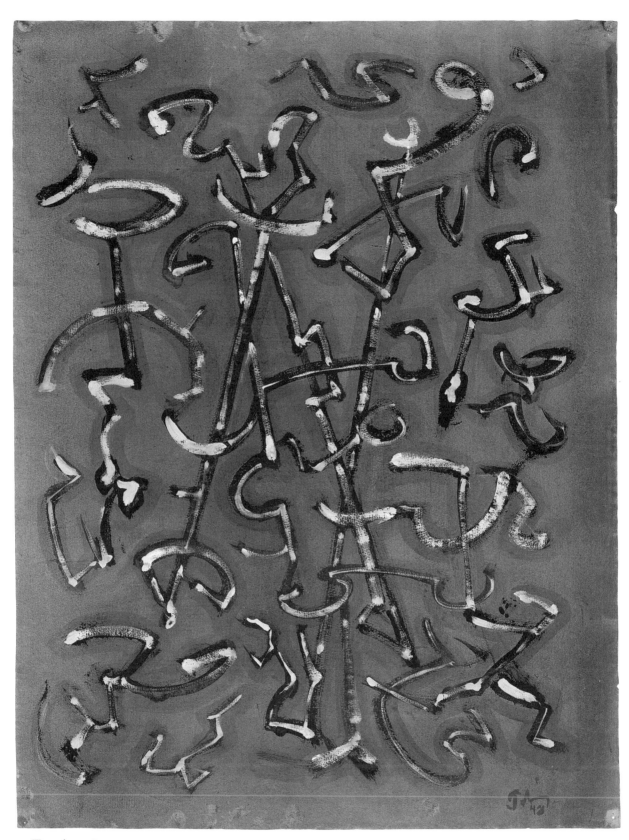

57. *Transit*, 1948

1918. Bahá'í beliefs influenced Tobey's art both in subject matter and in his choice of compositional format. In about 1962, Tobey explained the Bahá'í belief that "there has been but one religion, which renews itself under different names. The root of all religions, from the Bahá'í point of view, is based on the theory that man will gradually come to understand the unity of the world and the oneness of mankind."[6] It is this idea of universal human spirit that Tobey strove to express in abstract terms. Of his compositional format, Tobey wrote: "I've tried to decentralize and interpenetrate so that all parts of a painting are of related value.... I've hoped even to penetrate perspective and bring the far near."[7] Tobey's background, influences, and art all provide direct indications of both the common ground he shared with the Abstract Expressionists and the differences between them. Both his content and his formal elements find parallels with those of the New York based painters, who recognized these similarities and held Tobey in high regard. Like the Abstract Expressionists, Tobey sought to express humanity's oneness with the universe, and he did so via allover compositions of linear energy. However, although the tenets of Bahá'í led Tobey to similar subject matter, Tobey's allegiance to Bahá'í distances him from the Abstract Expressionists, whose conceptually based art was synthesized from diverse sources and did not follow any one belief system and whose starting point was in the most personal realms.

Tobey shared some important artistic sources with the Abstract Expressionists. Like them, Tobey took his art a step beyond European modernism. It is particularly pertinent that Paul Klee—whose small works convey multireferential content in allover formats—was directly influential on both Tobey and the Abstract Expressionists. Primary among the interests held in common by these American artists is that of Eastern art and ideas. Tobey had a lifelong involvement with the East. Beginning in the 1920s, he was intrigued by Asian art and philosophy. He first tried Chinese brush techniques in 1923, and in 1934, he spent about three and a half months in Japan, where he devoted himself to the study of painting and calligraphy. Tobey wrote about the importance of Japanese Zen art and ideas for himself and for American art of the 1940s: "Today the European influence is on the wane, and we are developing an indigenous style. However, we are growing more and more conscious of what I would term the Japanese aesthetic.... Several contemporary American artists have expressed an interest in Zen Buddhism with the

58. *Autumn Field,* 1955

implication that this has influenced their work, and the subject has been much discussed in the galleries and art journals."[8] The Abstract Expressionist whose paintings have the closest correspondences with Zen art and ideas is Ad Reinhardt, and Tobey's *Transit* of 1948 (fig. 57) shares many elements with Reinhardt's works of the late 1940s. Both artists invented their own calligraphic imagery hovering on atmospheric grounds, arriving at this similar vision almost simultaneously, more likely as the result of shared ideas and sources than through any direct influence on each other.

In March–April of 1957, Tobey made a series of fifty to ninety drawings with black Sumi ink on white paper. He was inspired by watching his Japanese artist-friends in Seattle. Sumi ink is made from compressed black soot that has been formed into sticks. When small amounts of the stick and water are mixed together, a thick creamy ink is created that can be diluted further with water. Although the Museum's untitled drawing from this series (fig. 60) is small in scale, its impact is considerable. It should be noted that other drawings from the series are nearly three by four feet in size. Ink is aggressively brushed and flung onto the page, a daring act for an artist in his late sixties who had always been more controlled in his process.

In 1954, Tobey described his white writing as a "performance, since it had to be achieved all at once or not at all."[9] In 1961, Tobey wrote that he experienced the desire to make Sumi drawings like "a kind of fever, like the earth in spring or a hurricane."[10] This stress on the act and spontaneity points to overlaps between Tobey's art and that of the gestural Abstract Expressionists. Indeed, the visual impact of Tobey's Sumi drawings is very similar to that of Jackson Pollock's black-and-white drawings of the early 1950s, such as the untitled work of ca. 1950 (see fig. 36), and of Robert Motherwell's *Lyric Suite* series of 1965 (see figs. 23–26).

Beginning in 1954, at least partially in reaction to the prominence that large-scale Abstract Expressionism had achieved, Tobey was pressured by both his New York dealer, Marion Willard, and his Paris dealer, Michel Tapié, to produce larger works.[11] Although he did enlarge the dimensions of his work somewhat, Tobey still filled these larger surfaces with the same small brushstrokes that characterized his smaller formats. Throughout his career, he steadfastly retained his preference for small size to envision cosmic breadth. He was not involved with the personally based vision of heroic humanity that is manifest in the Abstract Expressionists' use of

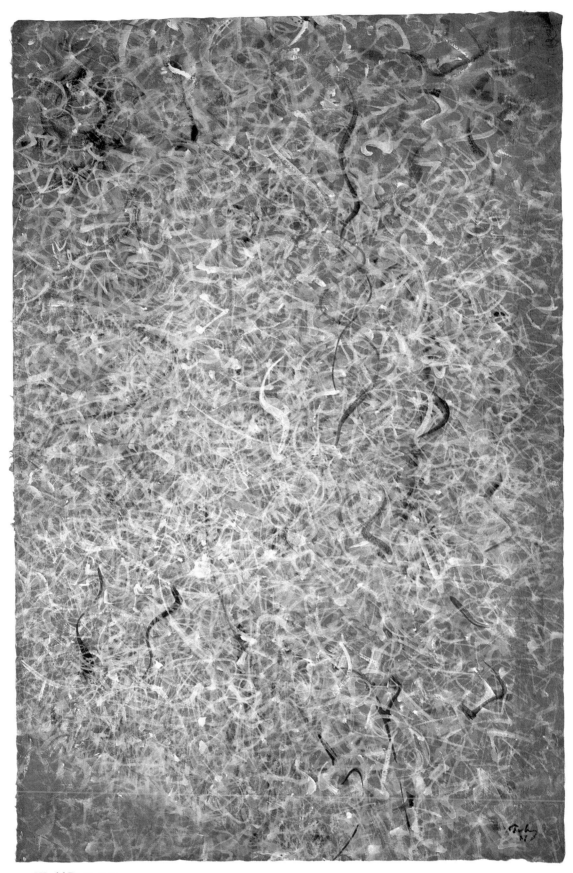

59. *World Dust*, 1957

enveloping environmental canvases. His more objective global view was a parallel but separate reaction to many of the same stimuli felt by the younger New York School painters. In July 1957, just a few months after making his Sumi drawings, Tobey said: "I know Kline exists and Pollock, but I have another note."[12]

1. Theodoros Stamos specifically sought out Tobey in Seattle in 1947, after seeing his pictures in New York.

2. Mark Tobey, quoted from Belle Krasne, "A Tobey Profile," *Art Digest* 26, no. 2 (October 15, 1951), p. 26.

3. Tobey created a large number of works during the 1940s and 1950s that were inspired by his reminiscences of New York City.

4. On the reverse side of this sheet, Tobey started, but never finished, another composition, with four geometrically stylized figures who are standing in a group and are dressed in elaborately patterned outfits (fig. 56a).

5. Tobey, quoted from John Russell, *Tobey,* exh. cat., Galerie Beyeler (Basel, 1966), n.p.

6. Tobey, quoted from an interview with Katharine Kuh; published in Katharine Kuh, *The Artist's Voice* (New York: Harper & Row, 1962), p. 240.

7. Ibid., pp. 237, 240.

8. Tobey, quoted from his essay titled "Japanese Traditions and American Art," *Mark Tobey,* exh. cat., Musée des Arts Décoratifs (Paris, 1961), n.p.

9. Tobey, quoted from Kuh, p. 240.

10. Tobey, quoted from a letter to Kuh, November 9, 1961; Kuh, p. 244.

11. See Eliza E. Rathbone, *Mark Tobey: City Paintings,* exh. cat., National Gallery of Art (Washington, D. C., 1984), p. 64.

12. Tobey, quoted from a letter to Marion Willard, July 1957; published in *Tobey,* Musée des Arts Décoratifs, n.p.

60. Untitled, 1957

Selected Bibliography

Note: This bibliography lists publications that either deal exclusively with works on paper or include them in the context of the artist's larger oeuvre. Because the sources in the notes at the end of each essay do not necessarily correspond with those in the bibliography, they are fully cited therein.

Alloway, Lawrence, and Mary Davis McNaughton. *Adolph Gottlieb: A Retrospective*. Exh. cat., Corcoran Gallery of Art, Washington, D.C. New York: The Arts Publisher, Inc., 1981.

Arnason, H. H. *Theodore Roszak*. Exh. cat., Walker Art Center. Minneapolis, 1956.

Arshile Gorky: Drawings to Paintings. Exh. cat., University Art Museum, University of Texas at Austin. Essays by Alice Baber, Hayden Herrera, Jim M. Jordan, Karlen Mooradian, Reuben Nakian, Harry Rand, and Ethel Schwabacher. 1975.

Arshile Gorky: Oeuvres sur papier 1929–1947. Essays by Erika Billeter, Bernard Blistène, Konrad Oberhuber, and Matthew Spender. Exh. cat., Musée cantonal des Beaux-Arts, 1990.

Ashton, Dore. "New York: Roszak, Draftsman." *Art Digest*, February 15, 1953, p. 16.

Boime, Albert. *Franz Kline: The Early Works as Signals*. Exh. cat., University Art Gallery, State University of New York, Binghamton, and Neuberger Museum, State University of New York, Purchase. 1977.

Cavaliere, Barbara, Mona Hadler, and Michael Preble. *William Baziotes: A Retrospective Exhibition*. Exh. cat., Newport Harbor Art Museum. Newport Beach, Ca., 1978.

Cavaliere, Barbara, and Theodore F. Wolff. *Theodoros Stamos: Works from 1945 to 1984*. Exh. cat., M. Knoedler Zurich AG. Switzerland, 1984.

Cernuschi, Claude. *Jackson Pollock: "Psychoanalytical" Drawings*. Durham: Duke University Press, 1992.

Clark, Trinkett. *The Drawings of David Smith*. Exh. cat., International Exhibitions Foundation. Washington, D.C., 1985.

Clearwater, Bonnie. *Mark Rothko: Works on Paper*. Introduction by Dore Ashton. New York: Hudson Hills Press, 1984.

Cummings, Paul. *Willem de Kooning: Drawings, Paintings, Sculpture*. Exh. cat., Whitney Museum of American Art. New York, 1983.

———. *David Smith: The Drawings*. Exh. cat., Whitney Museum of American Art. New York, 1979.

———. *20th Century Drawings from the Whitney Museum of American Art*. New York: Whitney Museum of American Art, 1987.

Dabrowski, Magdalena. *The Drawings of Philip Guston*. Exh. cat., Museum of Modern Art. New York, 1988.

D'Amico, Fabrizio. *Theodoros Stamos*. Exh. cat., Galleria Verlato. Milan, 1990.

David Smith, Drawings for Sculpture: 1954–1964. Exh. cat., Storm King Art Center. Mountainville, New York, 1982.

De Kooning Drawings. New York: Walker and Co., 1976.

Doty, Robert, and Diane Waldman. *Adolph Gottlieb*. Exh. cat., Whitney Museum of American Art. New York, 1968.

Faunce, Sarah. *Anne Ryan: Collages*. Exh. cat., The Brooklyn Museum. New York, 1974.

Flam, Jack. *Robert Motherwell, Drawings, A Retrospective, 1941 to the Present*. Exh. cat., Janie C. Lee Gallery. Houston, Texas, 1979.

Gaugh, Harry F. *The Vital Gesture: Franz Kline*. Exh. cat., Cincinnati Art Museum. New York: Abbeville Press, 1985.

Gibson, Eric. *Anne Ryan: Collages 1948–1954*. Exh. cat., Andre Emmerich Gallery. New York, 1979.

Glimcher, Marc, ed. *The Art of Mark Rothko: Into an Unknown World*. New York: Clarkson N. Potter, 1991.

Golding, John. *Arshile Gorky: Paintings and Drawings*. Exh. cat., The Arts Council of Great Britain. London, 1975.

Gordon, John. *Franz Kline: 1910–1962*. Exh. cat., Whitney Museum of American Art. New York, 1968.

Gorky Drawings. New York: Walker and Co., 1970.

Hess, Thomas B. *Barnett Newman*. Exh. cat., Museum of Modern Art. New York, 1971.

Hobbs, Robert, and Joanne Kuebler, *Richard Pousette-Dart*. Exh. cat., Indianapolis Museum of Art. 1990.

Hunter, Sam. *James Brooks*. Exh. cat., Whitney Museum of American Art. New York, 1963.

———. *Philip Guston: Recent Paintings and Drawings*. Exh. cat., The Jewish Museum. New York, 1966.

Jordan, Jim M. *Gorky Drawings*. Exh. cat., M. Knoedler & Co. New York, 1969.

Joyner, Brooks. *The Drawings of Arshile Gorky*. Exh. cat., University of Maryland. College Park, 1969.

Kingsley, April. *Adolph Gottlieb Works on Paper*. San Francisco: The Art Museum Association of America, 1985.

Kokkinen, Eila. *Drawings by Five Abstract Expressionist Painters*. Exh. cat., Massachusetts Institute of Technology. Cambridge, Mass., 1975.

Krauss, Rosalind. "Jackson Pollock's Drawings." *Artforum* (January 1971), pp. 58–61.

Larson, Philip, and Peter Schjeldahl. *De Kooning: Drawings/Sculptures*. Exh. cat., Walker Art Center, Minneapolis. New York: E. P. Dutton & Co., Inc., 1974. (traveling exh.)

MacNaughton, Mary Davis. *Adolph Gottlieb: Pictographs, 1941–1953*. Exh. cat., Andre Emmerich Gallery. New York, 1979.

Maurer, Evan M., and Jennifer L. Bayles. *Gerome Kamrowski: A Retrospective Exhibition*. Exh. cat., The University of Michigan Museum of Art. Ann Arbor, 1983.

Mooradian, Karlen. *An Exhibition of Drawings by Arshile Gorky*. Exh. cat., Oklahoma Art Center. Oklahoma City, 1973.

O'Connor, Francis V., and Eugene V. Thaw, eds. *Jackson Pollock: A Catalogue Raisonné of Paintings, Drawings, and Other Works*. New Haven: Yale University Press, 1978.

Osterwold, Tilman, and Lisa Mintz Messinger. *Jackson Pollock: Zeichnungen, Metropolitan Museum of Art, New York, Lee Krasner Stiftung*. Exh. cat., Württembergischer Kunstverein. 1990.

Philip Guston: Drawings 1947–1977. Exh. cat., David McKee Gallery. New York, 1978.

Pomeroy, Ralph. *Stamos*. New York: Harry Abrams, 1974.

Preble, Michael. *James Brooks: Paintings and Works on Paper, 1946–1982*. Exh. cat., Portland Museum of Art. 1983.

Preble, Michael, and Ethel Baziotes. *William Baziotes: Paintings and Works on Paper 1952–1961*. Exh. cat., Blum Helman Gallery. New York, 1988.

Rathbone, Eliza. *Mark Tobey: City Paintings*. Exh. cat., National Gallery of Art. Washington, D.C., 1984.

Richardson, Brenda. *Barnett Newman: The Complete Drawings 1944–1969*. Exh. cat., Baltimore Museum of Art, 1979.

Rose, Bernice. *Jackson Pollock: Drawing into Painting*. Exh. cat., Museum of Modern Art. New York, 1980.

———. *Jackson Pollock: Works on Paper*. Exh. cat., Museum of Modern Art and the Drawing Society. New York, 1969.

Schimmel, Paul, et al. *The Interpretive Link: Abstract Surrealism into Abstract Expressionism: Works on Paper 1938–48*. Exh. cat., Newport Harbor Art Museum. Newport Beach, Ca., 1986.

Sculptural Expressions: Seven Artists in Metal and Drawing 1947–1960. Exh. cat., Sarah Lawrence College Gallery. Bronxville, New York, 1985.

Seitz, William C. *Mark Tobey*. Exh. cat., Museum of Modern Art. New York, 1962.

Stebbins, Theodore E., Jr. *American Master Drawings and Watercolors*. New York: Harper & Row, in association with The Drawing Society, 1976.

Tuchman, Phyllis. *David Smith: Works on Paper 1953–1961*. Exh. cat., Salander-O'Reilly Galleries. New York, 1991.

Varian, Elayne H. *James Brooks: Paintings 1952–1975, Works on Paper 1950–1975*. Exh. cat., Martha Jackson Gallery. New York, 1975.

Waldman, Diane. *Mark Rothko, 1903–1970: A Retrospective*. Exh. cat., The Solomon R. Guggenheim Museum. New York, 1978.

———. *Twentieth-Century American Drawing: Three Avant-Garde Generations*. Exh. cat., Solomon R. Guggenheim Museum. New York, 1976.

Wechsler, Jeffrey. *Abstract Expressionism: Other Dimensions*. Exh. cat., The Jane Voorhees Zimmerli Art Museum, The State University of New Jersey, Rutgers. New Brunswick, 1989.

———. *Watercolors from the Abstract Expressionist Era*. Exh. cat., The Katonah Museum of Art. Katonah, New York, 1990.

Wysuph, C. L. *Jackson Pollock: Psychoanalytic Drawings*. New York: Horizon Press, 1970.

Index

Page numbers are in roman type. Page numbers on which illustrations appear are indicated in *italic* type.